THE MOVEMENT FOR THE
ACQUISITION OF ALL MEXICO
1846-1848

A Da Capo Press Reprint Series

THE AMERICAN SCENE
Comments and Commentators

GENERAL EDITOR: WALLACE D. FARNHAM
University of Illinois

THE MOVEMENT FOR THE
ACQUISITION OF ALL MEXICO
1846-1848

By
JOHN D. P. FULLER

DA CAPO PRESS • NEW YORK • 1969

A Da Capo Press Reprint Edition

This Da Capo Press edition of
*The Movement for the Acquisition of All Mexico,
1846-1848,* is an unabridged republication of
the first edition published in Baltimore in
1936 as Series LIV, Number 1, of the *Johns
Hopkins University Studies in Historical and
Political Science.*

Library of Congress Catalog Card Number 78-87545

Published by Da Capo Press
A Division of Plenum Publishing Corporation
227 West 17th Street
New York, N. Y. 10011

Printed in the United States of America

THE MOVEMENT FOR THE ACQUISITION
OF ALL MEXICO
1846-1848

THE MOVEMENT FOR THE ACQUISITION OF ALL MEXICO
1846-1848

By

JOHN DOUGLAS PITTS FULLER

Professor of History, Virginia Military Institute

BALTIMORE

THE JOHNS HOPKINS PRESS

1936

PRINTED IN THE UNITED STATES OF AMERICA
BY J. H. FURST COMPANY, BALTIMORE, MARYLAND

PREFACE

The writer desires to acknowledge his indebtedness to Dr.
W. S. Holt, whose valuable suggestions and constructive
criticisms have made possible the completion of this study.
Dr. A. K. Weinberg, of the Walter Hines Page School of
International Relations, has given freely of his time and
interest. Dr. Weinberg's help and his many suggestions as
to source material are greatly appreciated. The members
of Dr. Holt's seminar were always willing to lend their aid.
The writer's relationship with the late Dr. John H. Latané,
under whom he began his career as a graduate student of
history, has been a constant source of inspiration.

J. D. P. F.

CONTENTS

THE MOVEMENT FOR THE ACQUISITION OF ALL MEXICO
1846-1848

INTRODUCTION

This study is concerned with the movement for the absorption of all Mexico which became a force to be reckoned with in the United States during the latter part of the Mexican War. Among the expansionists of the period there were those who demanded only a portion of Mexico's territory and others who were primarily interested in Canada or Cuba. It has not been deemed necessary to consider the desire for parts of Mexico or for other territories except where such desire was involved in the development of the sentiment for all Mexico. The causes, as such, of the Mexican War also lie outside the scope of this account. To the extent, however, that the war was motivated by a desire for Mexican territory, its causes become part and parcel of the problem and must for that reason be examined.

There are many reasons why such a study as here proposed seems to be needed. Where the movement for all Mexico has received any attention at all, it has generally been treated as a minor factor in other developments in which the particular historian happened to be interested at the time.[1] Yet the subject is of sufficient importance to merit independent consideration. Expansionism has been one of the most important conditioning factors in the development of the United States and a study of the demand for all Mexico is psychologically illuminating for a better understanding of

---

[1] There is one short essay devoted exclusively to the attempt to absorb Mexico. This account, however, leaves much to be desired. Edward G. Bourne, " The Proposed Absorption of Mexico 1847-1848," *Annual Report of the American Historical Association for 1899*, I, 157-169. A summary of my own findings appeared under the title " The Slavery Question and the Movement to Acquire Mexico, 1846-48," *Mississippi Valley Historical Review*, XXI, 31-48.

American expansionism in general. Moreover, the imperialists and their program played an important part in the war itself. Since the desire for Mexico did not disappear at the end of the Mexican War, a knowledge of the movement in the forties furnishes a background for Mexican annexationism in the fifties and in later periods. It is of interest to know how the sentiment developed, by whom it was principally fostered, and the attitude of the administration and the various sections of the country toward it. Of particular importance should be an examination of the attitude of both the pro-slavery and anti-slavery interests, concerning whose policies considerable misinformation and obscurity still exist. Furthermore, the sentiment for the acquisition of Mexico is important in a consideration of the conclusion of the war. Finally, it is desirable to understand as fully as possible the reasons why the United States failed to absorb Mexico when the opportunity and temptation were so great.

A survey of the available evidence seems to indicate that the movement for the absorption of Mexico derived much of its strength from a manifest destiny sentiment which is related to the whole historical background of the American people. The expansionists were most numerous in New York and the West. Although the worship of manifest destiny was particularly widespread in these areas, there were many other motives of a decidedly more earthly character which caused the expansionists to look longingly across the Rio Grande. The slavocracy, though partly involved in the demand for Mexico, was not the chief element. In fact, in quarters where the attitude toward slavery was all-important there was, contrary to the accepted view, a definite " pro-slavery conspiracy " to prevent the absorption of Mexico and an " anti-slavery conspiracy " to take all Mexican territory that happened to be available. The expansionist sentiment as it developed after the outbreak of hostilities went through various stages of growth and affected the bringing of the war to a close. The apostles of empire were not able to write their program into international law for several reasons which have not been hitherto sufficiently recognized. Among these reasons was the fear of slaveholders that all Mexico would come into the Union as free territory, and also the fear of the sectional issue over slavery.

The writer realizes that many difficulties beset the task of a student of public opinion. There is among other things the problem of the measurement of the relative strength of different or opposing currents of sentiment. Confronted with the obvious impossibility of securing all or even a major portion of the evidence needed to construct a conclusive case, the investigator is forced to deal in probabilities which more often than not are open to serious question. Then too, there is that quality of human nature which leads men to sanctify their interests and desires by an appeal to the immutable laws of nature. What is published as a mandate of providential destiny is frequently no more than an attempted rationalization of motives which for one reason or another cannot be asserted without equivocation. The investigator is thus called upon to distinguish between real and professed motives. In a democracy partisanship inevitably colors the actions of politicians and their followers. The result is a glorification of the policy of one's own party and a distortion of the policy of the opponent. In short, the student is almost persuaded that public opinion, in the sense of a phenomenon which lends itself to generalizations of reasonable validity, is a figment of the imagination. Yet the task must be undertaken. It is hoped that the generalizations herein attempted will not be so erroneous as to be without value.

CHAPTER I

BACKGROUND

It must not be supposed that the desire for all Mexico was a product solely of the Mexican War. True it is that the war almost brought about the immediate absorption of Mexico by the United States, but the roots of the movement lie far back in the past. Interest in acquiring Mexican territory had been a factor in American history since the close of the Revolution. In general the development of that acquisitive spirit down to the outbreak of the Mexican War in 1846 naturally falls into three divisions: the first, from the independence of the United States to the Texan declaration of independence in 1836; the second, from the achievement of Texan independence to her annexation to the United States; the third, from the annexation of Texas to the beginning of the Mexican War.

Down to 1821 Mexico belonged to Spain, although from 1803 to 1821 the territory between the Sabine and Rio Grande Rivers was claimed by both Spain and the United States. During the Revolution Spain feared that if the thirteen colonies won their independence they might then attempt to overrun Mexico and other Spanish possessions.[1] This fear proved to be justified. Interest in acquiring Mexican territory seems to have first arisen in the United States largely as a result of resentment against Spain for obstructing free navigation on the Mississippi River. The frontiersmen of Kentucky and Tennessee were highly indignant with Spain for closing their best means of communication with the outside world. As early as 1786 a writer, whose article was published in the *American Museum*, suggested a rather drastic remedy:

. . . Two thousand brave Americans, under experienced officers, animated with resentment against those troublesome neighbors, [Spain] & having in object the conquest of the richest country in the

[1] Edward S. Corwin, *French Policy and the American Alliance*, pp. 105-120, 173-194.

world, would complete in a few wks., from their arrival at the Natchez, the red action of W. Fla., & La., in spite of all the Sp. efforts to resist us. Another army of about the same number of men, leaving the first conquerors to defend their new acquisitions at the expense of the same, would carry the war into the very heart of Mex. An expedition of this consequence would cost little or nothing to the U. S., & would insure to us, for ever, the free and undisturbed nav. of the Miss. . . .[2]

Here then is a proposal, sixty years before the Mexican War, which suggested the possibility of the conquest of Mexico.

In 1795 Spain agreed to open the Mississippi to American citizens.[3] The question was finally settled permanently by the purchase of Louisiana by the United States in 1803. Yet the expansionist ideas of the Southwest continued unchecked. The trek westward was gradually filling up the southwestern part of the United States with hardy adventurers who were not always willing to stop their advance at the borders of the United States but looked longingly toward Mexico. In 1804 an inhabitant of Kentucky wrote that the Kentuckians were "full of enterprise and although not poor, are greedy after plunder as ever the old Romans were, Mexico glitters in our Eyes—the word is all we wait for." [4] In 1806 Aaron Burr merely attempted to translate into fact the dreams of expansion cherished by the entire Southwest. Just how far Burr meant to go is not definitely known. At any rate he talked of an expedition against Mexico and won much support for the project among influential men in the West.[5] Burr's scheme failed, but the ideas on which its success was predicated continued to develop on the frontier. On the eve of the War of 1812 there was a lively interest in Mexico throughout the Southwest and a general opinion that she was ready to fall into American hands.[6] It was this lust for

---

[2] *American Museum*, III, 434-435.

[3] For a lucid summary of the importance of the struggle for the opening of the Mississippi and the negotiations leading to the treaty of 1795, see Arthur P. Whitaker, *The Spanish American Frontier: 1783-1795.*

[4] Quoted in Julius W. Pratt, *The Expansionists of 1812*, p. 62.

[5] On this subject, see Walter F. McCaleb, *The Aaron Burr Conspiracy.*

[6] Pratt, p. 12.

Mexico which partially explains the vigorous support of the war in the Southwest.[7] Nowhere did this feeling find clearer expression than in an article in the Nashville *Clarion* in April, 1812.

... Whilst our eastern and southern brethren are purchasing renown in arms, and extending the limits of this republic, are we condemned to remain inactive . . . ? No, citizens of the West! a destiny still more splendid is reserved for you. Behold the empire of Mexico, a celestial region. . . . Here it is that the statesman shall see an accession of Territory sufficient to double the extent of the republic. . . .[8]

That the plans of the Southwest for the conquest of Mexico failed to materialize was due largely to lack of general support for the enterprise. Mexico was only the extreme part of a general expansionist program which involved other Spanish territory in the South as well as British territory in the North. Sectional controversies and indifferent success in carrying on the war caused the entire fabric to fall to pieces.[9] But the advance into the Southwest continued and the expansive sentiment remained ready to flame forth on a more auspicious occasion.

In the meantime, the attention of the United States government and people was becoming centered on a smaller portion of territory claimed by Spain; that country lying between the Sabine and Rio Grande Rivers to which the name Texas was rather loosely applied. In its inception the Texas problem had little connection with the general southwestward movement. It soon, however, became a part of the main current. Since it was this same Texas which precipitated the set of conditions that led to the drive for all Mexico in 1847-1848, it will be necessary to examine the subject briefly at this point.

As a result of the vague description of the boundaries of Louisiana in the treaty which ceded that territory to the United States, Texas was claimed by both Spain and the United States. The merits of the controversy need not detain

---

[7] *Ibid.*, pp. 60-125.
[8] Quoted in *ibid.*, pp. 124-125.
[9] *Ibid.*, pp. 13, 238-274.

us here. Suffice it to say that by the Florida Treaty of 1819 the United States surrendered any claim she might have had to Texas. From the point of view of this study it is sufficient to note that the surrender of Texas displeased many Americans. The feeling that the United States had given up territory which was rightfully hers strengthened the desire for the "reannexation" of Texas when the chance came later.[10] And, after all, it was the "reannexation" of Texas which furnished the occasion for the Mexican War. As Mexico succeeded to the authority of Spain in 1821, Texas became a part of the independent Mexico. Under Mexican jurisdiction Anglo-American pioneers poured into Texas, thus making that country an outpost of American expansionist activity. It seemed an auspicious time for the United States to "repossess" Texas. Accordingly in 1827 and again in 1829 attempts were made to buy the whole or a part of Texas from Mexico. The net result of these efforts was nothing but an increased suspicion in the minds of the Mexicans that the United States had sinister designs on their territory.[11] A few years later the Americans in Texas undertook to decide their own destiny. Perhaps it was inevitable that Anglo-Saxons would not long remain satisfied under Mexican jurisdiction. Be that as it may, after a series of irritating incidents the Texans rebelled and declared their independence in 1836.[12] The first inroad on Mexican territory had begun. Where was it to end? The Mexican War would answer that question at least for the time being.

The years from 1836 to 1845 witnessed developments which boded ill for Mexico. The Texans having declared their

---

[10] Justin H. Smith, *The Annexation of Texas*, pp. 5-7.

[11] William R. Manning, *Early Diplomatic Relations between the United States and Mexico*, pp. 306-309, 334-345. The Mexicans had long been suspicious of the United States. In 1822 the first Mexican Minister at Washington wrote his government: "The haughtiness of these republicans will not allow them to look upon us as equals, but merely as inferiors; and in my judgment their vanity goes so far as to believe that their capital will be that of all the Americas." *Ibid.*, p. 279 n.

[12] Smith, pp. 9-13; George L. Rives, *The United States and Mexico, 1821-1848*, I, 182-361.

independence sought union with the United States, but for a time met failure.   They then developed a program of expansion which the shortsighted policy of Mexico tended to intensify.   As time went on the sentiment for the annexation of Texas became increasingly strong in the United States. Along with this desire for Texas, and closely related to it, there went a growth of general expansionist sentiment which looked far beyond Texas.   In 1845 when Texas was annexed to the United States, the expansionists in both countries joined forces and faced a Mexico who was still unwilling to make the concessions which her national safety demanded. Out of this situation the Mexican War emerged and the program of the most ardent imperialists in the United States came very near being pushed to completion.

The Texan expansion movement first appeared in the form of an attempt on the part of that republic to extend her boundaries to the Rio Grande River on the South and West.[13] Although the limits of Spanish Texas had been officially designated, there was some confusion about the western portion of the line.   An order of May 1, 1811, placed the boundary farther to the west than did an official map, prepared in 1816 to carry out the provisions of the order.   The details are not important.   It should be pointed out, however, that in any case the boundaries of Texas under both Spanish and Mexican rule did not extend farther to the southwest than the Nueces River, nor farther to the west than the point now forming the southeastern corner of New Mexico.   This line was nowhere nearer than fifty miles to the Rio Grande and in some places it was about four hundred miles away from that river.[14]

Here, then, is the origin of the controversy as to the proper limits of Texas.   The Texans were never able to establish occupation or control over the territory lying between Texas proper and the Rio Grande.   Nevertheless, by an act passed in December, 1836, the Congress of the republic declared that

---

[13] For a detailed study of Texan expansionism, see William C. Binkley, *The Expansionist Movement in Texas, 1836-1850.*

[14] *Ibid.,* pp. 1-11; George P. Garrison, *Westward Extension,* pp. 104-106.

the Rio Grande from mouth to source formed a part of the boundary of Texas.[15] For nine years Mexico steadily refused to recognize the fact the Texans had established control over any territory at all, thus making no distinction between the territory actually under the jurisdiction of Texas and that to which she merely asserted a claim. By the time the Mexicans were, or rather appeared to be, disposed to face the fact that the Texans had established an independent state, with territory bounded on the southwest by the Nueces River, Texas had become a part of the United States. Mexico now had to face the great North American republic, whose President fully intended to make good the entire Texan claim. It was an April day in 1846 that a collision between the troops of Mexico and those of the United States in the disputed area between the Nueces and the Rio Grande ushered in the Mexican War. The immediate occasion of the war, therefore, grew out of the fact that Texas as an independent power had claimed more territory than she had embraced under Mexican rule.[16]

The Texan quest for territory did not stop at the Rio Grande, but included other portions of Mexico as well. The ambitions of the young republic seemed to increase with time. Starting with a desire, rather vaguely expressed, to acquire territory on the Pacific Ocean, leading Texans were by 1842 thinking of acquiring Upper and Lower California together with a considerable portion of the remaining Mexican territory.[17] In the same year the Texan Congress passed an

---

[15] Binkley, pp. 43-67.

[16] *Ibid.*, pp. 123-141; Eugene I. McCormac, *James K. Polk*, pp. 373-414; Justin H. Smith, *The War with Mexico*, I, 138-150.

[17] Binkley, pp. 28-42, 118-122. In 1837 the Governor of Arkansas informed Secretary of State Forsyth of the United States that the Texan legislature " had . . . provided for the establishment of a [land] district embracing one entire county and a greater part of another belonging to Arkansas . . . and a land office under the control of the Texian Republic [was] to be forthwith established in the County of Miller in the State of Arkansas. . . ." George P. Garrison, ed., *Diplomatic Correspondence of the Republic of Texas*, in *Annual Report of the American Historical Association for 1907*, II, 230. The Texan Secretary of State admitted that the citizens of Miller County, Arkansas, had elected and sent members to the Congress of Texas,

act extending the boundaries of the republic so as to include more than half the territory of Mexico. President Houston, however, vetoed this amazing piece of legislation.[18] The veto did not meet with the approval of an appreciable part of the population of Texas. Houston's private secretary, Washington D. Miller, took up the gage for the expansionists. On February 16, he wrote Houston:

A great drama is in progress. Two acts have already passed. The first was the settlement and establishment of the independence of the United States—the second, the settlement and liberation of Texas—the third will be the conquest of Mexico.[19]

Miller did not stand alone, for, as the New Orleans *Commercial Bulletin* noted, the idea of conquering Mexico was quite general in Texas in 1842.[20] Although he had thwarted the plans of the Texan Congress, Houston had no misgivings about the future of his country when her wealth and population should warrant a career of expansion. Upon retiring to private life after his second term as president, Houston declared in his farewell message, December 9, 1844, that "if we remain an independent nation, our territory will be extensive—unlimited. The Pacific alone will bound the mighty march of our race and our empire. From England and America her soil is to be peopled." [21] It was the wretched financial condition of Texas added to the fact that the project of annexation to the United States soon took the center of the stage, which pushed the expansionist program into the back-

which members had been allowed to participate in legislation. Secretary Irion also confessed that a land district had been established to issue titles to land in Miller County under the authority of Texas. No further steps would be taken, however, until the boundary was settled. *Ibid.*, p. 242. Regardless of the merits of the question, it will be noticed that the Texans were not at all backward when it came to extending their jurisdiction in all directions over territory claimed by others. They had to be more cautious, however, in dealing with the United States than was necessary in dealing with Mexico.
[18] Binkley, p. 93. For Houston's amusing veto message in which he attempted to bring the Texan legislators back to earth, see Ephraim D. Adams, ed., *British Diplomatic Correspondence Concerning the Republic of Texas 1838-1846*, p. 603.
[19] Quoted in Binkley, p. 119.
[20] Smith, *The Annexation of Texas*, p. 51.
[21] Quoted in Binkley, p. 121.

ground. Three months after Houston's pronouncement in his farewell message the United States Congress consented to the annexation of Texas. A new accession of strength was about to be added to the forces making for expansion in the United States.

Expansionism in Texas was intimately connected with expansionism in the United States. It was President Jackson's intimation that the North and East would become reconciled to annexation if Texas could bring California along with her that caused the Texans to become interested in acquiring territory on the Pacific. When the annexation scheme languished, the Texans, led on by the beckonings of manifest destiny, became interested in securing a port on the Pacific to satisfy their own commercial requirements.[22] At the same time leaders in Texas were careful to point out the fact that the annexation of Texas would open up a marvelous field of expansion for the United States. Should the latter power fail to take advantage of her opportunities, a powerful Texan empire might ultimately be in a position to check the expansion of the United States.[23] This was an argument which could be counted upon to appeal to imperialists in the United States. After annexation the Texans became citizens of the United States and were involved in the sentiment for further Mexican territory. Houston and Rusk, as United States senators from Texas, were to be found in the front-line trenches of the expansionist cohorts in 1848. An examination of the course of events in the United States which culminated in the annexation of Texas will show that the Texans were not the only ones casting covetous eyes on Mexican territory.

Viewed from a distance the annexation of Texas represents nothing more than another step in that westward movement

[22] *Ibid.*, pp. 29, 220.
[23] Thomas J. Green, *Journal of the Texian Expedition against Mier*, pp. 387-388; A. J. Donelson to Calhoun, 8 January 1848, Chauncey S. Boucher and Robert P. Brooks, eds., *Correspondence Addressed to Calhoun*, in *Annual Report of the American Historical Association for 1929*, p. 421. Donelson is here describing the ideas Houston expressed in 1845.

which carried the Anglo-Saxon from the Atlantic to the Pacific. The movement into the Southwest was just as natural as the movement into the Old Northwest—a part of the same phenomenon. Proximity and similarity of geographical conditions caused the South to be particularly interested in Texas. That interest represented no diabolical conspiracy against the free states. The decade 1830-1840, however, saw the beginning of the anti-slavery crusade which threw the South on the defensive. Since agitation at the North made it appear that the failure to acquire Texas would be a victory for the abolitionist forces, the South very naturally became interested in preventing such a victory. Had there been no slavery in the United States the annexation of Texas would probably have been accomplished ten years sooner than it actually was.[24] The nature of the struggle between 1836 and 1845 has been very aptly indicated by George P. Garrison:

With the progress of sectionalization the pro-slavery element became ever more anxious to secure Texas, and the anti-slavery element to exclude it from the Union; but neither of these was for a time strong enough to control its own section, and, when the issue came, the instinct of expansion finally cast the balance in favor of Texas.[25]

It will serve no useful purpose to trace again the course of events which culminated in the accomplishment of annexation. The work has already been thoroughly done.[26] Certain features, however, are interesting in view of subsequent developments. The appetite of the expansionists increased as it was fed. Moreover, it was the annexation of Texas with an undetermined boundary which gave the apostles of empire a fighting chance to put their program into effect immediately.

The desire to obtain Texas was more natively a product of the West rather than of the South.[27] In the West, too, there

---

[24]Chauncey S. Boucher, *In Re that Aggressive Slavocracy*, pp. 13-28.
[25] *Westward Extension*, pp. 96-97.
[26] Smith, *The Annexation of Texas*. See also, Ephraim D. Adams, *British Interests and Activities in Texas, 1838-1846*, and Jesse S. Reeves, *American Diplomacy under Tyler and Polk*.
[27] Smith, *The Annexation of Texas*, p. 108. See also, Thomas Scott

appeared a lively sentiment for additional territory in 1844 and 1845. Judge Scott, of the Ohio Supreme Court, assured Calhoun that the West stood "Heart and Soul" for the annexation of Texas, and for "securing every foot of land west of the Rocky Mountains to which we can assert a just claim."

The whole country drained by the Gulf of Mexico from the Sabine to the Rio del Norte [said Scott] is essential for the perfect security of Western and Southern interests and those interests will be greatly promoted by the establishment of our title to the country west of the Rocky Mountains to such an extent along the shores of the Pacific Ocean as will secure a sufficient number of good Harbors on that Ocean. . . .[28]

The most powerful newspaper in Illinois frankly recommended that if the Texas controversy led to war between the United States and Mexico, it should not end "until the empire of Mexico, as well as Texas, is added to the territory of the Union; and the broad continent only limit the domains of the United States from east to west." [29] "The United States must possess California" said the Chicago *Democrat*, in March, 1845.[30] Apparently there was not everywhere a great deal of respect for the territorial integrity of the republic below the Rio Grande.

During the debates on annexation in Congress, western Democrats displayed the expansive sentiments common to their section. Douglas, of Illinois, "was one of those who believed that there was nothing to fear from the acquisition of freemen to the States of this Union, or of territory to this republic . . ." While not favoring unjust methods, Douglas "would use all legal means to extend the territory of this republic from the Atlantic to the Pacific . . ." [31] Owen, of Indiana, thought that the province of federal legislation

---

to Calhoun, 4 April 1844, and William Hale to Calhoun, 18 May 1844, *Correspondence Addressed to Calhoun*, pp. 220-221, 231-232.

[28] Scott to Calhoun, 4 April 1844, *Correspondence Addressed to Calhoun*, pp. 220-221.

[29] Illinois *State Register*, 27 December 1844, quoted in William E. Dodd, "The West and the War with Mexico," *Journal of the Illinois State Historical Society*, V, 163.

[30] *Ibid*.

[31] *Congressional Globe, 28th Cong., 2d sess.*, p. 97.

would contract " as our territory expands." The past proved that this expansion would come, " and safely, yes, most beneficially may this Union and its blessings spread over the entire continent of North America." [32]   Speaking of the annexation of Texas, Bowlin, of Missouri, said:

> Another matter that gives peculiar importance to this question is, that it is a question of the enlargement of territory, by which the area of civil and religious liberty is to be spread out and extended. We may vainly fancy that we may check the progress [of] emigration by refusing to extend our institutions and our laws, commensurate with its progress. But it is a vain delusion; our people, with a spirit of enterprise unparalleled in the history of man, are pushing onward, scattering in their train the blessings of enlightened liberty; you may follow them with your laws and institutions, which they love and cherish with a patriotic devotion, and thereby add strength and permanent glory to the republic; or you may, under the influence of a contracted policy, refuse, and lose an empire in extent, and all the political advantages, which the acquisition of such a country, must necessarily bring with it.[33]

Although these speakers had in mind the immediate problem of the annexation of Texas, they were incidentally creating a state of mind and furnishing catchwords which could be used to further any scheme of expansion.

While they seemed to be most numerous in that section, the West did not contain all the prophets of expansion. A southern Whig asserted that it should be the policy of the United States to own " all the cotton lands of North America if we can." [34]   Belser, an Alabama Democrat, informed the House of Representatives that it was impossible to limit " the area of freedom—the area of the Anglo-Saxon race." Another half century " would hear the song of the American reaper on the shores of the Pacific." Although Houston's threat to conquer Mexico had been much ridiculed, the member from Alabama warned his colleagues that " its accomplishment was not so improbable as some persons supposed." If Mexico persisted in claiming sovereignty over Texas, and continued her unjust treatment of the Texan

---

[32] *Ibid.*, p. 112.
[33] *Ibid.* (Appendix), p. 93.
[34] Richard Hawes to Calhoun, 21 March 1844, *Correspondence Addressed to Calhoun*, pp. 217-218.

people, "the day was not far distant when the declaration of the Texian President would prove itself to be true." [35] As a matter of fact, and sooner, probably, than Belser expected, the "declaration of the Texian President" did come true, but the Texans had the help of the United States in their adventure against Mexico. Senator Merrick, of Maryland, contended that the annexation of Texas was "no ordinary act of legislation." It was "a subject which concerned the fate of empires, and which was to affect for weal or for wo through ages yet to come, millions of the Anglo-Saxon race." [36] To the charge that annexation was a sectional measure in the sense that it would increase the power of the South, Rhett, of South Carolina, replied "that he should like to know how any addition of territory was ever to be made that was not sectional in that sense."

Will you [continued Rhett] ever get territory that surrounds the whole Union? . . . The question was, whether the limits of our Union were to stand as now, and never to be extended; or whether we are to go on and extend the blessings of our free institutions over a vast territory; whether we are to go on as our ancestors intended, enlarging our possessions, extending our institutions, and fulfilling our high destinies, or remain as we are. If Texas was to be the last acquisition that we are to make, there might be some force in the objection; but it was not the last. He could not tell, with the improvements which have been made in machinery and steam navigation, how long it would be before the whole continent was brought under the blessings of our constitution. [37]

Had Rhett been able to foresee the future he would probably have been more than willing that Texas should be the "last acquisition" to be made by the United States. A representative of the northeastern Democracy in the House, Charles J. Ingersoll, of Pennsylvania, discovered that the natural boundary between the "Anglo-Saxon and the Mauritanian races" was the desert lying between the Nueces and the Rio Grande Rivers. While a state of peace existed, that boundary would be "sacred," but otherwise "one or the other race, must be conquered, if not extinguished." [38] The state of peace was destined to last just about five months longer. If

[35] *Cong. Globe, 28 Cong., 2d sess.*, p. 88.
[36] *Ibid.*, p. 321.   [37] *Ibid.*, p. 167.   [38] *Ibid.*, p. 86.

Ingersoll were correct either the Mexicans or the Anglo-Saxons were in a precarious condition. One may guess that in Ingersoll's opinion it was the Mexicans who were in danger.

The proposed annexation of Texas brought forth a demand for the annexation of Canada to redress the balance of power between the slave states and the free states. Senator Dickinson, of New York, on February 3, 1845, presented a petition from a group of northerners " praying for the annexation of the Canadas, in case of the annexation of the Mexican province called Texas." The New Yorker frankly confessed, however, that he " did not sympathize very strongly with the petitioners." [39] On the same day Senator Porter, of Michigan, presented a petition from citizens of Detroit which also demanded the acquisition Canada. The petition recited the commercial and military advantages of Canada, whose annexation was needed in order to act as a counterweight for Texas. The project was declared to be " vitally connected with the permanent prosperity of the North, the glory of the whole nation and the perpetuity of our free institutions." [40] These maneuvers amounted to nothing more than an indirect attack on the annexation of Texas, as Porter, himself, admitted.[41] Nevertheless, there was a genuine interest in the acquisition of Canada and a belief that she might not long remain under British sovereignty.[42] This belief represented a state of mind which was symptomatic of the American disease of the period.

It appears, then, that even before the annexation of Texas there had developed in the United States a noticeable sentiment for expansion. It found its supporters chiefly in Democratic ranks and was stronger in the West than in any other portion of the country. It was a sentiment vaguely thought of and vaguely expressed, drawing its emotional appeal from an ideal of manifest destiny.[43] In the West the

[39] *Ibid.*, p. 232.
[40] *Ibid.* (Appendix), p. 151.
[41] *Ibid.*, pp. 151-154.
[42] See for instance the New York *Herald*, 6 January 1846; speech of Stephen A. Douglas, *Cong. Globe, 29th Cong., 1st sess.*, pp. 258-259.
[43] For an illuminating study of manifest destiny, see Albert K.

devotees of manifest destiny were particularly numerous.[44] Along with idealistic factors there were other factors more realistic and sordid, such as the desire of the South to get control of all the cotton lands of North America and the demand of commercial interests for a harbor on the Pacific Ocean. These ends could be achieved only at the expense of Mexico. It was not the intention or the desire of many of the expansionists to absorb Mexico. Indeed, for the most part the sentiment for all Mexico took the form of a feeling that the ultimate absorption of Mexico was inevitable rather than a demand for immediate action. Yet in following out their special aims, various groups among the expansionists let loose forces which could not easily be controlled. Those who wanted Texas, those who wanted California, those who wanted California and Texas, and those who would not object to taking all Mexico while they were about it worked together up to a certain point. The annexation of Texas was the first step. This might not have led to war had it not been for the desire to get California. It now remains to be seen how the annexation of Texas added to the desire for California helped produce a situation in which the champions of all Mexico had their opportunity.

The actual achievement of the annexation of Texas not only furnished the occasion for the Mexican War, but it also further stimulated the expansionist sentiment which had been developing during the preceding decade.[45] The joint resolu-

---

Weinberg, *Manifest Destiny: a Study of Nationalist Expansionism in American History.* See also, Ephraim D. Adams, *The Power of Ideals in American History,* pp. 65-94.

[44] Frederick J. Turner, *The Frontier in American History,* pp. 213-214. As Professor Julius W. Pratt has shown, the term " manifest destiny " was first used by John L. O'Sullivan, of New York, editor of the *Democratic Review,* in the number for July-August, 1845. There was a second appearance of the expression in the New York *Morning News,* 27 December 1845. This, too, may be attributed to O'Sullivan. After this date " manifest destiny " became a catchword for the expansionists. Julius W. Pratt, " John L. O'Sullivan and Manifest Destiny," *New York History,* XIV, 222-225. But the idea of manifest destiny existed before the phrase was coined, especially in the West. As will later appear, however, the followers of the providential theory of empire were also very numerous in New York.

[45] It should be pointed out that the controversy with Great Britain

tion for the admission of Texas was signed by President Tyler on March 1, 1845, just three days before the end of his term of office. By July 4, Texas had completed the process by which her acceptance of the terms laid down in the resolution was to be recorded. It was not until December, however, that she formally became a part of the United States. From the time when the public first considered that annexation was certain until the outbreak of the Mexican War, numerous articles and speeches speculating on the signs of the times appeared in the press. It was evident from the tone of the press and in private correspondence that Texas was considered as only the harbinger of greater things to come.

The Texans had hardly been formally ushered into the Union when northeastern observers began to elaborate their views on the implication of the event. The *New Englander*, of New Haven, discussed the annexation of Texas as an "index of the future policy of the United States." This rather conservative journal, with anti-slavery leanings, thought that "the idea of limiting the jurisdiction of the nation to a smaller territory than the whole of North America, is now abandoned perhaps forever." In all probability, either by force or voluntary union, the territory of the United States would eventually include "all that lies north of the isthmus of Darien." To this idea the *New Englander* gave qualified approval:

And we are free to confess that if such a consummation could be brought to pass, without national dishonor, without public crime, we should regard it with the highest satisfaction. It would at once extend religious freedom to every part of North America, and give a predominant influence to the Protestant cause.[46]

The New York *Herald* asserted that the popularity of annexation was astounding. The people were "puzzling their brains to find out new countries to annex." It was the "stepping

concerning Oregon, which was rapidly approaching a crisis at the time of the annexation of Texas, gave additional impetus to the general sentiment for expansion. The Democratic platform of 1844 had contained a pronouncement in favor of Oregon as well as Texas, both projects thereby gaining additional support. For the details of the Oregon controversy, see McCormac, pp. 555-611.

[46] *New Englander*, IV, 149.

stone to popularity, now to invent some new annexation scheme." [47] A prominent Democratic politician of New York expressed the desire for California and all Mexico, so that an isthmian canal might be constructed "between the two great Oceans." [48] The *Herald*, itself, independent in politics, advocated the annexation of all Mexico instead of California alone.[49] The *Democratic Review* declared:

Is there one who does not hope for—nay does not foresee . . . that the future is to extend to all the people of the American continent, if true to their trust, institutions based upon the light of reason and truth, upon the benefits and inherent and equal rights of all men, and upon that fraternal bond of union which alone can give promise of universal peace.[50]

One can hardly say that the imperialists were lacking in assurance. It is only one step, and not a very long one at that, from hope and prophecy to action.

In Maryland and the South, California, Cuba and Oregon furnished themes for public and private pronouncements. *Niles' Register* and the Baltimore *American*, both Whig organs, interpreted the omens as being very unfavorable to Mexico. All Mexican citizens should know, said the former, that if they submitted to the annexation of Texas it would only "invite a new dismemberment, already avowed—that of California." [51] In like vein was the comment of the *American*:

There must be some uncertainty as to the course of Mexico until the result is known. If that republic shall not determine upon war it will be because of her consciousness of weakness. For Mexico knows very well that the acquisition of Texas by the United States is but the beginning of acquisitions by which her territory is to be rent from her. . . . There are now in California thousands of American settlers, and every year is adding to the number. . . . But Mexico will gain nothing by war. She would only accelerate her own downfall by it. . . .[52]

---

[47] From an article signed " G. M. D.," New York *Herald*, 1 January 1846.

[48] F. W. Byrdsall to Calhoun, 26 January 1846, *Correspondence Addressed to Calhoun*, p. 321.

[49] New York *Herald*, 20 January 1846.

[50] *Democratic Review*, XVIII, 64.

[51] *Niles' Register*, LXVIII, 17.

[52] Baltimore *American*, quoted in *ibid.*, p. 18.

Ex-President Tyler thought that with England's aid the United States might be able to acquire California in return for concessions in regard to Oregon.[53]   In December, 1845, Senator Levy, a Florida Democrat, introduced in the Senate a resolution requesting the President to open negotiations with Spain for the purchase of Cuba. This was too much, and the next day Levy was persuaded to withdraw his resolution.[54] William Gilmore Simms, of South Carolina, expressed in poetry the current faith in the destiny of the United States:

> To keep us from our conquests, it requires
> That we be conquer'd! . . .
>
>   . . .
>
> As well attempt Niagara on the leap,
> With all her oceans, plunging o'er the steep,
> As hope to stay the torrent which moves on,
> Steady and still increasing as it flows,
> Destined to sweep the wastes of Oregon,
> And in Canadian wilds to melt their fettering snows.[55]

Although Simms had the Oregon dispute in mind the sentiment expressed was of general application. There was no more reason why the current should " sweep the wastes of Oregon " than sweep the wastes of Mexico. There was much more likelihood that the United States would be conquered in the former adventure than in the latter. At any rate it was Mexico that met the inundation and not Oregon.

To western expansionists, also, the annexation of Texas pointed the way to other acquisitions. With the end in view of stimulating interest in Cuba, a public meeting was held at Springfield, Illinois, on December 12, 1845. The gathering was addressed by the Democratic governor of the State.

---

[53] John Tyler to his son, 23 December 1845, Lyon G. Tyler, *The Letters and Times of the Tylers*, II, 449.

[54] *Cong. Globe, 29th Cong., 1st sess.*, pp. 92, 96. On the subject of Levy's resolutions an eastern paper declared: " He [Levy] intended, simply to plant a seed in early springtime—so that through the course of a warm and growing summer, it might grow and be ready for the sickle by harvest. . . . The movement that ended in the annexation of Texas . . . commenced in a similar, unpretending, jeering and laughable way. . . . Mr. Levy knew what he was about, and the people also knew what Mr. Levy was about. Both are crammed full of knowledge." New York *Herald*, 3 January 1846.

[55] *Democratic Review*, XVIII, 94.

Another meeting had been held in Springfield on a former occasion, the governor reminded his listeners. The result of that meeting was the annexation of Texas. Such would be the effect of the present meeting on the ultimate fate of Cuba. Having delivered himself of these sentiments, Governor Reynolds passed on to the climax:

Let that western spirit continue to act, let the American people spread themselves over the continent of North America, carrying with them the principle of freedom and Democratic institutions, and ultimately extend the blessing of civil and religious liberty over the whole earth, beginning with the island of Cuba.[56]

A group of Missouri Democrats expressed the hope that the annexation of Texas would be followed " by the spread of our free institutions, in due time, westward to the Pacific." [57] Whatever else may be said about the westerners, they certainly did not have a restricted outlook. One wonders how these champions of expansion could have occupied themselves after they had extended the " blessing of civil and religious liberty over the whole earth."

More realistic was the attitude in Louisiana, where there was considerable interest in California. An article in *De Bow's Review* described the many commercial advantages of that country with its fine harbors and strategic location " between the fur trading parts of North-West America, and the fisheries of the Southern Ocean." According to De Bow, if California were left to herself she had "little prospect beyond a nervous imbecility," but to " great commercial nations " she would " always be attractive." [58]   In other words, California in the hands of Mexico had no future, but in the hands of a nation like the United States her destiny, and incidentally the destiny of the United States as well, would be glorious. The New Orleans *Picayune* had no patience with the attempt to acquire Cuba because it " cast a certain amount of ridicule upon those other efforts at

[56] Illinois *State Register*, 2 January 1846.
[57] W. C. Anderson and others to Calhoun, 6 November 1845, *Correspondence Addressed to Calhoun*, p. 308.
[58] *De Bow's Review*, I, 66.

acquisition which are recommended by sound policy and overruling public necessities." [59]   The *Picayune* evidently considered the acquisition of Mexican territory as being in accord with the public interest.   To drive his point home, the editor declared that both England and France had designs on Mexico and the unsettled state of affairs between the United States and Mexico furnished a fertile field for European intrigues.[60]   Did it not also furnish a fertile field for American intrigues?

The annexation of Texas is thus seen to have stimulated by its example the desire for expansion in all directions.   The situation in January, 1846, was described by the New York *Herald*:

> The final annexation of Texas, effected by this Congress, and the re-occupation of the whole of Oregon, now under animated debate, comprehending also a movement looking North towards the whole of British North America—looking South towards Cuba, San Domingo, California, nay the whole of Mexico—all point to the accomplishment of a destiny which is dazzling while it is terrible.[61]

Many citizens of the United States were gradually becoming accustomed to the idea of empire.   More and more they were thinking, not only of Texas and Oregon, but also of Canada, Cuba, California and the rest of Mexico.   The expansionist sentiment as it manifested itself in 1846 was very complex and the various elements do not lend themselves to rigid classification.   Along with vague dreams of an empire of continental proportions there existed at the same time and often in the same mind a more definite interest in Cuba, California and all Mexico.   Much of this had in itself no immediate significance, but is illustrative of a tendency so characteristic of the " Roaring Forties."   To motives for expansion already noticed there had been added a desire to extend Protestant Christianity, a demand for a ship canal and an inclination to frustrate alleged machinations of European powers.   The chief seats of the imperialists were

---

[59] New Orleans *Picayune*, 3 January 1846.
[60] *Ibid.*, 10 January 1846.
[61] New York *Herald*, 10 January 1846.

in New York and the West. So far as the West is concerned, manifest destiny was apparently the principal exciting force behind the expansionists. While there was also much support for that theory of empire in New York, commercial and industrial considerations were seemingly of at least as much significance. If the eastern expansionist movement as a whole is considered, it appears that economics was stronger than emotion. This distinction would become more obvious in 1847 and 1848.

It is significant to note in connection with the fate of Mexico, that on the eve of the Mexican War there was a widespread interest in the acquisition of California present in all sections of the United States. The expansionist sentiment was far from being a peculiar prepossession of slaveholders. There were slaveholding expansionists to be sure, but, speaking generally, one might say that most of the strongholds of expansionism were located in the free states. It was also felt that because of the unsettled state of affairs between the United States and Mexico after the annexation of Texas there was some chance of getting California in the near future. Many of those affected with the general expansionist fever would support any scheme whatever for the acquisition of more territory. Practically all would welcome any measure designed to acquire California. At the same time President Polk was making efforts to reach an agreement with Mexico and get California. The result of his maneuvers would be the Mexican War.

The proposition that Polk precipitated the Mexican war in order to acquire California cannot be maintained with any degree of certainty. Yet his desire to add that territory to the United States cannot be overlooked in any investigation of the causes of the war. There is evidence that the President had determined shortly after his inauguration that the acquisition of California was to be one of the outstanding achievements of his administration.[62] Interest in territory along the Pacific was greatly stimulated by the receipt of

---

[62] McCormac, p. 351.

information at Washington in July, 1845, which seemed to indicate that England and France had designs on California.[63] The state of relations existing between Mexico and the United States apparently furnished an opening for efforts to get California. For years citizens of the United States had held valid claims against Mexico for which no satisfactory provision had been made.[64] It was a well-known fact that the only compensation Mexico could offer would of necessity have to take the form of territorial concessions.[65] Under the terms of the joint resolution for the admission of Texas into the Union, all questions of boundary which should arise with other nations were to be settled by the United States.[66] The American claims, the poverty of Mexico and the question of the Texas boundary might be used to advantage in furthering the expansionist aims of the President of the United States.

But on March 6, 1845, two days after Polk's inauguration, Mexico had severed diplomatic relations with the United States as a protest against the passage of the resolution for the annexation of Texas.[67] It was necessary that the wire to Mexico be mended before anything could be done, and, less than a month after he became President, Polk directed his efforts toward inducing Mexico to receive an envoy from the United States. On March 28, W. S. Parrott was commissioned as confidential agent in Mexico. His task was to endeavor to reach high officials of the Mexican government and persuade them to renew diplomatic intercourse with the United States.[68] Some months later information from Mexico convinced the Washington authorities that she was willing to receive an envoy from the United States. Accordingly, John Slidell was sent to Mexico.[69]

[63] James Buchanan to Thomas O. Larkin, 17 October 1845, John B. Moore, ed., *The Works of James Buchanan*, VI, 276; McCormac, pp. 385-387; Adams, *British Interests and Activities in Texas*, pp. 234-264.

[64] Smith, *The War with Mexico*, I, 74-81.

[65] *30th Cong., 1st sess., S. Doc. No. 52*, p. 75.

[66] *Cong. Globe, 28th Cong., 2d sess.*, pp. 362-363.

[67] *29th Cong., 1st sess., S. Doc. No. 1*, pp. 38-39.

[68] Buchanan's *Works*, VI, 132-134; McCormac, pp. 383-384.

[69] McCormac, pp. 384-385.

Slidell's instructions, dated November 10, 1845, show that Polk, although anxious to acquire New Mexico and California, did not intend to attempt to force Mexico to make the cession.[70] Slidell was informed that California was a " subject of vast importance to the United States, which will demand your particular attention." As much as twenty-five million dollars, in addition to the assumption by the United States of claims of its citizens against Mexico, could be offered for the cession of New Mexico and California as far south as Monterey. Smaller amounts would be given for New Mexico alone or for New Mexico and a smaller portion of California.[71] If, however, the Mexicans would not surrender any of New Mexico west of the Rio Grande or California, Slidell was authorized to assume the payment of claims if Mexico would recognize the Rio Grande from mouth to source and thence due north to the forty-second degree of north latitude as the boundary between the two countries.[72] In short, if Mexico would agree to submit to the annexation of Texas with the Rio Grande boundary she could keep California for the time.[73] Mexico refused, however, even to receive Slidell and to a certain extent she is responsible for what followed.[74] After a four months stay in Mexico, and after the repeated refusals of two different governments to

---

[70] Slidell's instructions are printed in *30th Cong., 1st sess., S. Doc. No. 52*, pp. 71-80.

[71] *Ibid.*, pp. 78-79.

[72] *Ibid.*, p. 78.

[73] Polk had already conceived the idea that California might be acquired in much the same manner as in the case of Texas. On October 17, 1845, Buchanan wrote Larkin, American consul at Monterey: " Whilst the President will make no effort and use no influence to induce California to become one of the free and independent States of this Union, yet if the people should desire to unite their destiny with ours, they would be received as brethren, whenever this can be done without affording Mexico just cause of complaint." Buchanan's *Works*, VI, 277; McCormac, p. 387.

[74] The reason given by the Mexican authorities for refusing to receive Slidell was that they had agreed to receive a special commissioner and not a regular minister. It is possible, though not probable, that Polk suspected this. At any rate, the real reason for the failure to receive Slidell seems to have been the fact that the Mexican government feared for its existence if a representative of any sort was received from the United States. McCormac, pp. 384-385, 392-393; Smith, I, 96-98.

receive him, Slidell demanded his passports on March 17, 1846, leaving Mexico on March 21.[75]   After the rejection of his envoy, Polk was convinced that it would be necessary to wage war with Mexico in order to obtain a settlement.   It had already been decided in a cabinet meeting that the President should recommend war measures to Congress when events on the Rio Grande actually began the conflict.[76]

In January, 1846, while the result of Slidell's mission was still in doubt, General Taylor, who was stationed at Corpus Christi on the Nueces, was ordered to advance to the Rio Grande.   On April 12, Ampudia, the Mexican general in command on the Rio Grande, ordered Taylor to retire beyond the Neuces.   If the withdrawal did not take place within twenty-four hours, Ampudia declared that it would "clearly result that arms and arms alone must decide the question; and in that case, I advise you that we accept the war to which, with so much injustice on your part, you provoke us. . . ."   After this pronouncement Taylor blockaded the Rio Grande and prevented supplies from reaching Matamoras. Ampudia made no hostile move, however, and Taylor considered it doubtful that such a move would be made at the time.   Finally, on April 24, a party of dragoons sent out by Taylor "to watch the course of the river above on this bank, became engaged with a very large force of the enemy, and after a short affair, in which some sixteen were killed and wounded, appear to have been surrounded and compelled to surrender. . . ."   "Hostilities may now be considered as commenced," wrote Taylor to the War Department.[77]   News

[75] *29th Cong., 1st sess., S. Doc. No. 337*, pp. 61, 67; McCormac, pp. 390-404; Smith, I, 91-101.
[76] Milo M. Quaife, ed., *The Diary of James K. Polk*, I, 343, 354, 384-386.
[77] *29th Cong., 1st sess., S. Doc. No. 337*, pp. 123-125; McCormac, pp. 409-413; Smith, I, 145-150. It is interesting to note that Ampudia, by ordering Taylor to retire beyond the Nueces, seemed to admit that the presence of the American army as far as the Nueces was justified. In a similar vein was a proclamation, copies of which were circulated among the American soldiers by General Arista: "It is to no purpose if they tell you that the law for the annexation of Texas justifies your occupation of the Rio Bravo del Norte, for by this act they rob us of a great part of Tamaulipas, Coahuila, Chihuahua, and New Mexico. . . ."   John R. Kenly,

of this affair having reached Washington, Polk, who had already determined to recommend war to Congress, immediately sent a message to the legislators on May 11. Mexico was represented as having invaded the United States and having " shed American blood on American soil." [78] American blood had been shed truly enough, but that was about the only thing which was certainly true. In record time, however, a bill recognizing a state of war was rushed through Congress. On May 13, it was declared that " by the act of the Republic of Mexico, a state of war exists between that Government and the United States." The President was authorized to call for fifty thousand volunteers and ten million dollars was appropriated to carry on the war.[79]

In Congress the Whigs, generally speaking, were willing to vote supplies of men and money to carry on hostilities but they opposed the preamble which declared that the war existed by the act of Mexico. It was intimated, and no doubt politics was involved, that Polk had been responsible for beginning hostilities when he ordered Taylor to advance to the Rio Grande.[80] Rather than incur the odium of being thought unpatriotic most of the Whigs, in spite of their alleged distaste for the preamble, voted for the bill which stated that Mexico had begun hostilities. Only fourteen members of the party in the House and two in the Senate had the hardihood to record their votes in opposition to the war.[81] No Democrat voted against the bill, but Calhoun, of South Carolina, the great pro-slavery leader, refused to vote at all because " he was not prepared to affirm that war existed between the United States and Mexico, and that it existed by the act of that government." [82] Benton, of Missouri,

---

Memoirs of a Maryland Volunteer in the War with Mexico, pp. 40-41. It is legitimate to suspect that such broadsides were intended merely to paint the United States in still blacker colors.

[78] For Polk's message, see James D. Richardson, ed., *Messages and Papers of the Presidents*, IV, 437-443.

[79] *Statutes at Large*, IX, 9-10.

[80] For speeches of Garrett Davis, of Kentucky, in the House, and of Berrien, of Georgia, and Crittenden, of Kentucky, in the Senate, see *Cong. Globe, 1st sess., 29th Cong.*, pp. 794-795, 801, 802.

[81] *Ibid.*, pp. 795, 804.   [82] *Ibid.*, pp. 796-797.

was also disposed to be recalcitrant but finally surrendered and voted in support of the administration.[83]   The most vigorous support of Polk's policy and the war came from western Democrats such as Houston, of Texas, and Cass, of Michigan.[84]   Perhaps the opportunity for which the westerners had been waiting had now arrived.

An analysis of the vote in Congress shows that the Mexican War was a Democratic war in the sense that the only votes cast against it came from Whig sources.   The actual tabulation of votes, however, is not sufficient to show opinion on the war.   Among the Democrats, Calhoun refused to vote one way or the other and the Van Burenites in private expressed sentiments critical of the administration and the war.[85]   Motives were mixed and the exigencies of politics determined the attitude of many Democrats and Whigs.   The Whigs did not forget the political possibilities of a situation

---

[83] *Ibid.*, pp. 798, 804.

[84] For speeches of Houston and Cass, see *ibid.*, pp. 798, 801.   The Washington correspondent of a southern newspaper declared that the war party proper consisted wholly of Democrats, who were very much chagrined at the course the Oregon negotiations were taking. " Of course," continued the writer, " they have recovered fresh hope and confidence, and now look to the conquest of California. . . . War is their policy.   War with somebody, anybody, so that it presents the prospect of personal eclat and territorial aggrandizement." Charleston *Mercury*, 18 May 1846.   The *Mercury* was undoubtedly prejudiced against the westerners, but some time later a southwestern journal declared that " there are in the country, and especially in the West, a great many dissentients from the terms of the Oregon treaty who will acquiesce therein, if the result of our operations upon the Pacific should secure to us the possession of the bays of St. Francisco and Monterey."   New Orleans *Picayune*, 1 July 1846. Evidently there was some truth in the story of the *Mercury's* correspondent.

[85] A few days after the declaration of war Senator Dix, of New York, wrote Van Buren: " In fact I fear the Texas fraud is carried out to its consummation by a violation of every just consideration of national dignity, duty & policy. . . . But I know this is high treason, and, therefore, desist."   Dix to Van Buren, 16 May 1846, Van Buren MSS.   For similar letters, see Cambreleng, Gilpin and Law to Van Buren, 16, 24 May 1846, 22 August 1847, *ibid.*; Aulting to Donelson, 29 March 1847, Donelson MSS.   Very complicated, however, were the motives of the Van Burenites.   Entirely aside from the merits of the case, the followers of Van Buren resented the fact that Polk secured the nomination in 1844 instead of their own leader.   They were, therefore, prone to assume the rôle of conscientious objectors to every act of the Polk administration.

in which they could criticize the Democratic administration for having begun the war, and at the same time demonstrate their patriotism by voting supplies to protect the American army.[86] Although all the votes in opposition came from the region north of Maryland, the war was not a slaveholder's affair.[87] Many of its most ardent supporters like Cass came from the free states, while pro-slavery Calhoun's attitude was very similar to that of the Whigs. Moreover, the Southern Whigs who made up a majority of the slaveholders and owned from two-thirds to three-fourths of the slave property in the entire South, although voting for the war, spent the next two years accusing Polk of having precipitated hostilities and opposing the acquisition of Mexican territory.[88]

Who was the aggressor in this series of events leading to the Mexican War and what rôle was played by the desire for Mexican territory? As to who was the aggressor in the actual conflict, it appears that the American President must bear a considerable portion of the credit or discredit for the first collision.[89] Mexico may have desired war as did Polk, himself, after the failure of Slidell's mission. War might have come in any event, but, after all it was Taylor's march to the Rio Grande which gave the Mexicans an excuse to begin hostilities, and it was that general's blockade of the river that amounted to the first overt act of war. If Polk really thought that Mexico had agreed to receive Slidell, and he apparently did, then he gave the Mexicans an honorable means of escape from their difficulties without the loss of California. The President may have been justified in assuming the Rio Grande to be the boundary of Texas, but it is legitimate to suspect that his desire for California made him all the more anxious to uphold the rights of the United

[86] Smith, I, 181-187.
[87] In the House there were five negative votes from Massachusetts, five from Ohio, and one each from Maine, Rhode Island, New York and Pennsylvania. In the Senate Davis, of Massachusetts, and Clayton (Thomas), of Delaware, furnished the only negative votes. *Cong. Globe, 29th Cong., 1st sess.*, pp. 795, 804.
[88] On the attitude of slaveholders, see Arthur C. Cole, *The Whig Party in the South*, pp. 104-134; Boucher, pp. 30-39.
[89] McCormac, pp. 409-414. For a contrary view, see Smith, I, 150-155.

States. In other words, the American President, for reasons which he chose to consider sufficient, took certain steps which precipitated the Mexican War, as a result of which war he fully intended from the beginning to acquire California. In his policy toward Mexico and his desire for Mexican territory Polk did not stand alone, but had the support of thousands of his countrymen, especially in the West. It was later to be demonstrated that many were willing to go much further in their designs on Mexico than was the Chief Executive.

In 1846, then, there began a war which was destined to bring to a culmination, for the time being, forces which had been developing in the United States since the American Revolution. From 1783 to 1836 interest in acquiring Mexican territory was confined principally to the Southwest and was motivated first by hostility to Spain, and later by the expansive tendencies of Americans on the frontier. From 1836 to 1845 further interest in expansion was generated by the continued westward advance of the frontier, the long discussion on the question of the annexation of Texas, and the controversy with Great Britain concerning Oregon. During this period there can be noticed the growth of a feeling of nationalism, a desire to increase the power of the nation by territorial expansion, and a feeling that the United States was destined to extend its sway over the whole of North America. This would bring the blessings of enlightenment and democratic principles of government to the benighted peoples of the continent. At the same time other motives for expansion besides this ideal of manifest destiny became evident. Among them were the desire of the commercial interests for a harbor on the Pacific Ocean, a desire to control all the cotton lands of North America, and a desire to prevent European expansion in the new world. In 1845 the annexation of Texas added to the United States a population already enamored with the idea of taking Mexican territory and furnished the occasion for the Mexican War. This war, caused to some extent by the general desire for California, would give the forces of expansion which had been developing so long a chance to display their strength in concrete fashion.

CHAPTER II

EMERGENCE

Until the fall of 1847 the demand for Mexican territory extended no further than the acquisition of Upper California and New Mexico. At the very beginning of the war, however, there appeared expressions of more extended ideas of expansion, very general in some cases, in others more specifically relating to Mexico. But not until the fall of 1847 did these ideas become widespread. Three fairly well-defined stages may be noticed in the development of the sentiment for all Mexico before October, 1847. There was at the outbreak of the war a sudden outburst of expansionist sentiment which looked toward all Mexico, but this soon died down, or at least ceased to receive vocal expression. There was general approval for the acquisition of California,[1] but the plans of the administration were not definitely known. For the first five or six months of the war, therefore, public interest was centered on the task of finding out just what territory the President would attempt to secure. By October, 1846, it was apparent to the public that California at least would become a part of the United States. But the war did not come to an end as quickly as was expected and Mexico rejected overtures for peace in the fall of 1846. Public opinion began to demand more drastic measures. There were frequent intimations that it would be in order to demand more territory from Mexico and if that country still refused to listen to reason it was declared that her existence as a separate nation would be endangered. Finally, beginning in the spring of 1847 after notable victories of the American forces in Mexico, there can be noticed an increasing tendency to believe that the war could end only in the absorption of all Mexico, not so much an avowed demand as a strong conviction which was

---

[1] Contemporaries were not very exact in their use of the term "California." The demand for California generally included territory north of a line from some point on the Rio Grande due west to the Pacific. This would include the whole or a part of New Mexico. The chief interest, however, was in California.

39

in many cases, no doubt, created by an ardent desire to acquire Mexico. In the meantime, the issue as to whether or not slavery should exist in territory acquired from Mexico had assumed an ominous character. But by October, 1847, when developments in connection with the war seemed to point toward the absorption of Mexico, some of the explosive material in the slavery question had been removed. The way was thus prepared for the development of larger ideas of expansion.

Immediately after the outbreak of hostilities there were indications in widely scattered parts of the country of a spirit that could mean disaster to Mexico if the war continued a sufficient length of time for it to develop. Caleb Cushing, a Massachusetts Democrat, disclaimed any desire " to witness the extinction of Mexico," but asserted that by beginning the war she had " dared the worst; and the result may be . . . the complete dissolution and extinction of the Mexican Republic." [2] The editor of the New York *Herald* thought that the war might be looked upon " as the commencement of a vast, a terrible, a magnificent future." It might " lay the foundation of a new Age, a new destiny, affecting both this continent and the old continent of Europe." [3] The meaning of this oratory became more clear when the New York paper undertook to advise Polk as to the proper course of procedure in case he intended to annex Mexico. Shortly afterwards the *Herald* assured the public that even if the United States did acquire vast stretches of territory, republican institutions would not thereby be endangered.[4] The *Democratic Review* asserted that the " task of the American people for the present century, is clearly to take and occupy the northern continent of America." Mexico had caused a war " which in itself must hasten the occupation of the whole continent by the people of the United States." [5] There was apparently no clear expression of sentiment for the immediate absorption

[2] *Democratic Review*, XVIII, 439-440.
[3] New York *Herald*, 13 May 1846.
[4] *Ibid.*, 9, 15 July 1846.
[5] *Democratic Review*, XIX, 85-86.

of Mexico in the Northeast. But the possibilities in the situation created by the war were distinctly recognized. Given time this recognition of a possibility might readily develop into a direct demand for all Mexico.

Manifest destiny sentiments continued to display their accustomed energy in the West, which was stimulated somewhat by the presence of war. On June 16, McClernand, a Democrat of Illinois, in a brief résumé of the history of the westward movement declared in the House that the people of the United States were " destined to overflow the continent, irrigating it for the growth and predominance of liberty." [6] According to " Dow Jr.," writing in the Illinois *State Register*, the Mexicans " are reptiles in the path of progressive democracy—who, with his big boots on is bound to travel from Portland to Patagonia—and they must either crawl or be crushed." [7] Editorially the *Register* argued that the Mexican War presented an opportunity " for the prosecution of our glorious mission," which ought not be allowed to pass " unimproved." [8] The New Orleans *Commercial Bulletin* was convinced " that the war, if prosecuted with the least spirit, will lay the foundation for, if it do not immediately produce, the entire overthrow of Mexico, and its incorporation into the Federal Union. . . ." [9] It was not to be expected that the West, where belief in the manifest destiny of the United States was one of the articles of faith, would be very reluctant to advance the designs of Providence by taking possession of all Mexico if the opportunity should arise. Had not the Mexican War created an excellent opportunity for carrying out the " civilizing mission " of the United States?

In the early stages of the conflict representative Democratic newspapers in the Southeast confined their editorial comments to urging a vigorous prosecution of the war and asserting its just character.[10] They did not display the ex-

[6] *Cong. Globe, 29th Cong., 1st sess.*, p. 984.
[7] Illinois *State Register*, 17 July 1846.
[8] *Ibid.*, 10 July 1846.
[9] New Orleans *Commericial Bulletin*, quoted by Richmond *Enquirer*, 12 May 1846.
[10] See for examples Richmond *Enquirer*, 13, 21 May 1846; Nashville *Union*, 16 May 1846; *Southern Literary Messenger*, XII, 452.

pansive sentiments of the North and West. The Charleston
Mercury, supporter of Calhoun, was even somewhat dubious
about the justice of the war and declared that after the
Mexicans had been driven across the Rio Grande the war
might end " if Congress were not a little daft." [11] In view of
the contention of anti-slavery Whigs that the Mexican War
had been precipitated by pro-slavery interests with the direct
purpose of extending the area of slavery, it is passing strange
that such an ardent supporter of slavery as the Charleston
Mercury should have evinced so little enthusiasm concerning
the Mexican War. The truth is, that Southeastern slaveholders were never very enthusiastic supporters of extensive
annexations of Mexican territory. As will appear later their
enthusiasm became less evident as the war progressed and
the acquisition of an increasing amount of Mexican territory
became more and more probable.

Whether the sentiment for general expansion expressed
at the beginning of hostilities would become strong enough
to threaten the existence of Mexico would be disclosed during
the later course of the war. In the meantime expressions of
extended ideas of expansion died down. Doubtless a desire
for large additions of territory remained, but the interest of
everybody concerned—the administration—Congress—and the
people seemed to be centered on concrete proposals as to the
amount of territory to be taken from Mexico. When one
considers the display of expansionist sentiment before the
war and immediately after the beginning of hostilities it
appears that the immediate demands for Mexican territory
were comparatively moderate.

The President and members of his cabinet had plans,
though they were not very definite, regarding territory to be
acquired from Mexico from the very outset of the war. There
was, however, some divergence of opinion concerning the
amount to be taken. On May 13, Secretary of State, Buc-

---

[11] Charleston *Mercury*, 15, 18 May 1846. One reason why certain
elements in the Southeast disapproved of the war was a belief that
it would produce a high tariff. Boucher, *In Re that Aggressive
Slavocracy*, p. 35.

hanan, suggested in a cabinet meeting that foreign governments be notified that in going to war the United States " did not do so with a view to acquire either California or New Mexico or any other portion of the Mexican territory." Fear of the action of England and France if satisfactory assurances on the subject of the objects of the war were not given to those powers seems to have been the ostensible motive of the Secretary of State. The intervention of European powers had no terrors for Polk, who insisted that though the United States had not gone to war for conquest,

yet it was clear that in making peace we would if practicable obtain California and such other portion of Mexican territory as would be sufficient to indemnify our claimants on Mexico and to defray the expenses of the war which that power by her long continued wrongs and injuries had forced us to wage.

Buchanan's was a voice crying in the wilderness. He stood alone in the cabinet and on May 14 a communication sufficiently ambiguous to provide for most eventualities was sent to foreign powers.[12] The President may or may not have gone to war for conquest. But the conclusion is almost inescapable that had there been no California there would have been no Mexican War, at least at the time it actually occurred. Perhaps Polk was not so very sorry that Mexico had "forced" the United States to wage war.

During May and June the administration gave further attention to the subject of territorial indemnity from Mexico. Polk meant to acquire California, New Mexico and other northern provinces of Mexico if possible. He would prefer to secure all the territory north of a line beginning at the mouth of the Rio Grande due west to the Pacific, but failing that would accept as a minimum Upper California and New Mexico.[13] Buchanan was afraid of the slavery question if any territory were taken south of a boundary formed by the Rio Grande to the thirty-second parallel of north latitude and

---

[12] Polk's *Diary*, I, 396-399, 400. For a copy of the dispatch, see Buchanan's *Works*, VI, 484-485.
[13] Polk's *Diary*, I, 437-438, 495-497.

thence along that parallel to the Pacific.[14]   This Pennsyl-
vanian could not afford to take a position which might ruin
his political fences back home.   Robert J. Walker, of Mississippi, Secretary of the Treasury, was the expansionist par
excellence of the cabinet.[15]   At the end of June Walker was
ready to take all the territory north of a line from the mouth
of the Rio Grande due west to the Pacific.[16]   He would
later be found advocating the acquisition of all Mexico along
with the turncoat Buchanan.   The Secretary of the Navy,
George Bancroft, of Massachusetts, wrote on June 22: " If
Mexico makes peace this month the Rio del Norte and the
parallel of 35° may do as a boundary: after that 32° which
will include San Diego." [17]   The other members of the cabinet generally agreed with the President.[18]

Within two months, then, after the beginning of the Mexican War, the administration had a tentative program of expansion worked out.   The President had decided that the
United States must have at least New Mexico and Upper
California, but he wanted more territory and had not com-

[14] *Ibid.*, pp. 495-497; Buchanan to General James Shields, 23 April
1847, Buchanan's *Works*, VII, 286-287.   Since the beginning of the
war the Oregon controversy had been settled.   This rendered English
interference in the Mexican embroglio less likely.   It is probable,
however, that the Secretary of State feared the unfavorable reaction
of northern public opinion fully as much as the intervention of foreign powers when he exhibited such moderate ideas on the subject
of Mexican territory.
[15] Dodd, *The West and the War with Mexico*, pp. 160-161, 163,
165, 171.
[16] Polk's *Diary*, I, 495-497;   Elwood Fisher to Calhoun, 24 September 1846, *Correspondence Addressed to Calhoun*, p. 360.   Walker was
generally recognized as one of the leading expansionists of the
country.   Although living in Mississippi at this time, Walker was
born and reared in Pennsylvania and he was never identified with
the pro-slavery interest.   Later on, the accusation was made that
Walker was a traitor to the interests of the South.   The Secretary
of the Treasury seems to have acquired the expansive spirit of the
Southwest and to have desired to create new states imbued with free
trade ideas.   Dodd, pp. 160-161, 163, 165, 171; H. Donaldson Jordan,
" A Politician of Expansion: Robert J. Walker," *Mississippi Valley
Historical Review*, XIX, 362, 377-379; Boucher, p. 36; New Orleans
Picayune, 22 July 1846.
[17] Bancroft to Samuel Hooper, 22 June 1846, M. A. De W. Howe,
ed., *The Life and Letters of George Bancroft*, I, 291.
[18] Polk's *Diary*, I, 437-438.

mitted himself against acquiring other provinces of Mexico. Secretary Walker would doubtless have been glad to secure all Mexico in June, 1846. At any rate Polk could count on his support in any scheme for annexing territory—the more the better. Buchanan seems to have been the most moderate expansionist of the cabinet during the first months of the war. But his ideas would be determined with reference to public opinion. The Secretary of State would oppose nothing which he was convinced had popular support and more particularly the support of Pennsylvania. As yet, however, neither the President nor any member of his cabinet had definitely expressed a desire for all Mexico, but a door had been left open through which they might pass on the way to the absorption of that country.

While the administration was maturing its plans of conquest the same question was being mooted in Congress and in the press. Whig members of the national legislature charged the Democratic administration with having provoked a war for territorial acquisitions, perhaps for the conquest of all Mexico. Either directly or by implication the Whigs expressed a pious disapproval of territorial conquests.[19] In reply, the Democrats asserted that no one desired the conquest or annexation of Mexico, and that the war was being waged merely to force Mexico to meet her just obligations. It was a well-known fact that Mexico could satisfy her obligations only by a cession of territory, but Democratic congressmen were somewhat hesitant when it came to fixing the exact amount of territory which should be required. They confined themselves to such vague generalizations as "indemnity for the past and security for the future" and "justice" from Mexico.[20] There was only an occasional reference to the manifest destiny of the United States.[21] The Democratic

---

[19] For speeches of Stephens, of Georgia, Webster, of Massachusetts, and Giddings, of Ohio, see *Cong. Globe, 29th Cong., 1st sess.*, pp. 982, 1015, 1095.

[20] For speeches of Smith, of Indiana, Yancey, of Alabama, and McClernand, of Illinois, see *ibid.*, pp. 910, 983-984.

[21] See for instance remarks of Levin, of Pennsylvania, and McClernand, *ibid.*, pp. 964, 983-984.

press, however, in all parts of the country called for the acquisition of California in payment for claims against Mexico
and the expenses of the war.[22]   An avowed demand for all
Mexico was conspicuous by its absence.   But if the principle
of indemnity for the past including the cost of the war were
to be followed in making a settlement, who could tell where
the demand for territory would stop.   In fact a principle had
been announced which under the stress of circumstances
could be and was finally used to justify the absorption of the
southern republic.

The attitude of the Charleston *Mercury,* representing the
Calhoun wing of the Democratic slaveholders, is interesting.
As early as May 20, the Charleston daily stated that there
"would have been no war if the United States had left the
narrow and worthless valley of the Rio del Norte to Mexico." [23]
A few days later the *Mercury's* editor expressed alarm at
current tendencies:

We shrink with dread from the development of a love of conquest
among our people.   Such a passion is the enemy of liberty and law.
A military republic will in the very nature of things ever tend to a
dictatorship and thence to a monarchy.   What do we look for, even
in the acquisition of all Mexico to compensate us for the corruption
and overthrow of the Republic?   Let us take caution in time.   Let
us not cast away the priceless jewel of freedom, for the lust of
plunder and the pride of conquest.[24]

Thus a leading Democratic newspaper in perhaps the most
extreme pro-slavery section of the Union began to fight
against a tendency which it was thought might lead to the
union of Mexico and the United States.

Nevertheless, the signs of the times did point to the annexation of considerable portions of Mexican territory to the
United States.   Events in July and August, 1846, convinced
the public that the President intended to acquire at least
New Mexico and Upper California.   The occupation of these
territories by the American forces and the proclamations of

---

[22] For examples, see Nashville *Union,* 28 May 1846; New Orleans
Picayune, 1 July 184ʳ; Illinois *State Register,* 10 July 1846; New
York *Herald,* 27 July 1846; Richmond *Enquirer,* 8 October 1846.
[23] Charleston *Mercury,* 20 May 1846.
[24] *Ibid.,* 25 May 1846.

the military commanders to the inhabitants seemed to indicate that Polk did not intend to restore the provinces to
Mexico.[25]   Also, on August 8, the President asked Congress
for a special appropriation "for the purpose of settling all
our difficulties with the Mexican republic." [26]   It was obvious
that the money was to be used to induce the Mexicans to
surrender a portion of their territory, probably California
and New Mexico.   Polk did not get his appropriation but
his apparent intention of securing Mexican territory evoked
favorable comment from leading editors who seemed to think
that California was already a part of the United States.[27]
Probably that was only the first step in the dismemberment
of Mexico.

The President's attempt to secure money from Congress to
further his schemes of expansion was a notable event in connection with the movement for the absorption of Mexico.
Then it was that the slavery issue appeared on the scene.
Certain northern Whigs declared that the Mexican War had
resulted from a desire to extend and maintain the institution
of slavery.[28]   It was a northern Democrat, however, who
actually introduced the issue into Congress.   When White, a
Whig of New York, intimated that the purpose of Polk's
request for a special appropriation was to extend the area
of slavery, the Democrat Wilmot, of Pennsylvania, partly in
answer to White's challenge, offered an amendment to the
appropriation bill which provided that slavery should not
exist in any territory acquired from Mexico.[29]   Wilmot's
Proviso failed along with the bill and as Congress adjourned
on August 10, there had not been enough discussion on the

---

[25] A copy of Sloat's proclamation to the Californians and Kearny's
proclamation to the inhabitants of New Mexico may be found in
Niles' Register, LXXI, 83, 87-88.

[26] *Cong. Globe, 29th Cong., 1st sess.*, p. 1211.

[27] Boston *Post*, 5 October 1846; Detroit *Free Press*, 15 October
1846; New Orleans *Picayune*, 6 October 1846; Nashville *Union*, 23
October 1846; Richmond *Enquirer*, 8 October 1846.

[28] For instance Joshua R. Giddings, *Cong. Globe, 29th Cong., 1st
sess.* (Appendix), pp. 641-645. See also, *New Englander*, IV, 432.

[29] *Cong. Globe, 29th Cong., 1st sess.*, pp. 1214, 1217-1218. For the
proceedings in Congress, see McCormac, *James K. Polk*, pp. 441-443.

subject to arouse the passions of the pro-slavery and anti-slavery forces. During 1847, however, the slavery question was destined to cause the expansionists much difficulty in mapping out their plans for the acquisition of Mexican territory.

During the first few months of the Mexican War, then, there was little or no public expression of a sentiment for the acquisition of all Mexico. In some quarters, especially in the North and West, there were assertions to the effect that the United States was destined to include the whole of North America and that the Mexican War would probably hasten the accomplishment of that destiny. But there was little indication of a desire for the immediate consummation of that great design. A belief that the United States was destined to control the whole of North America, however, could very easily be translated into a desire to acquire all Mexico if circumstances seemed to warrant such a program. The Democratic party, moreover, was committed to the policy of exacting indemnity from Mexico for the claims of American citizens and for the expenses of the war. While the cession of California might be considered as satisfactory indemnity in September, 1846, the total expense of the war would increase as long as hostilities continued. In the end it might require all the Mexican territory to pay the expenses of the conflict.

Meanwhile, the war was not redounding to the greater glory of the United States. Greatly exaggerated ideas of Mexico's wealth had been noised abroad and it was thought that only one swift campaign would be necessary to conquer a nation of Indians, negroes and degenerate Spaniards, who would disperse at the first volley of the lordly Anglo-Saxons.[30] But such did not seem to be the case. After five months of war Mexico had not been conquered. Military victories had been won but the American soldiers were not yet, in September, 1846, " revelling in the Halls of the Montezumas." This was peculiarly exasperating in view of the contempt with which the Anglo-Saxon regarded the lowly Mexican. The

---

[30] Smith, *The War with Mexico*, I, 125-126.

tendency of any armed conflict to bring to the surface the less admirable qualities of human nature made its influence felt by greatly intensifying the impatience and irritation of the American people. Finally, late in September news came that Mexico had virtually refused Polk's offer to negotiate a peace.[31] Consequently it is not surprising that demands for a more vigorous prosecution of the war and for more drastic terms of peace made their appearance.

In New England, the Boston *Post* declared that if Mexico continued to refuse peace the United States must prosecute hostilities " to win a decisive battle, which must either end the war or else end the Mexican republic." In any case the Sierra Madre Mountains rather than the Rio Grande should be the boundary between the United States and Mexico.[32] " O. P. Q." thought that if Mexico failed to show a " returning sense of justice," the American flag would probably be unfurled over the whole Mexican republic.[33] " John Smith Jr., of Arkansas," wrote that Mexico would " probably fight to the last, and in the end realize a fate that many years ago befel [sic] Poland." [34] Even the *New Englander* began to support territorial expansion. At the beginning of hostilities, this anti-slavery organ condemned the war as a shameful attempt to extend slavery.[35] Six months later, however, the editor was convinced that the war might " result in great good to the world—to this country—to Mexico herself—to the cause of learning, good government and religion." California and New Mexico were in the hands of the United States and would probably " be incorporated into our union." " It is, we think," continued the *New Englander*, " one of the advantages of this extension of our boundaries, and one which will engage the attention of our statesmen; that it will open to us, in a narrower part of the continent, a way to the Pacific Ocean." [36] Backed by a combination of ethics and economics, imperialist sentiment could become very strong indeed.

---

[31] McCormac, pp. 441-442, 444-447.
[32] Boston *Post*, 9 December 1846.
[33] *Ibid.*, 22 October 1846.
[34] *Ibid.*, 30 November 1846.
[35] *New Englander*, IV, 432.
[36] *Ibid.*, V, 141-142.

Mexican obstinacy created a similar reaction in New York. The *Herald* urged that the war be prosecuted more vigorously. The United States should have as indemnity when peace was secured all the territory north of a line drawn from the intersection of the Rio Grande with the thirtieth degree of north latitude west to the Gulf of California. Mexico should also be required to give a bond, "secured by a mortgage on the richest portion of her territory," to keep the peace.[37] It was apparent to the *Democratic Review* that the Mexican race "must amalgamate and be lost, in the superior vigor of the Anglo-Saxon race, or they must utterly perish." The Mexicans might "postpone the hour for a time, but it will come, when their nationality shall cease." The editor of the *Review* contended that the war could be ended only by the seizure and occupation of all the large cities in Mexico and the complete overthrow of the Mexican army. If the United States would do this, at the same time guaranteeing security of person and property, the growth of commercial and industrial interests would eventually cause the regeneration of Mexico.[38] It is not likely, however, that the "regenerated" Mexico would have been independent.

The omens also indicated increased expansionist sentiment in the domain of the southeastern Democracy. The Nashville *Union* ridiculed the "antiquated and *obsolete ideas* of the federal party on the subject of territorial acquisition," which were appearing in the Whig papers. "The principles of free government," said the editor, "are destined to progress and to extend, and in due time they will be diffused over all Mexico." The *Union*, however, deemed it necessary to call attention to the fact that the Mexican population was not yet ready "for the enjoyment of national freedom under our system of government."[39] "The most dire result of all wars," said another editor, "is where one nation destroys the existence of another, annihilates its Government, and holds it as a conquered province." It was hoped that this "fearful

---

[37] New York *Herald*, 29 September 1846.
[38] *Democratic Review*, XX, 100-101.
[39] Nashville *Union*, 23 October 1846.

alternative" would not be forced upon the United States. "Yet necessity would justify even this—a fool-hardy refusal to make a proper peace, the non-existence of a responsible government, might drive us to such procedure."[40] On December 17, 1846, Wilson Lumpkin, a Georgia Democrat wrote Calhoun:

. . . nothing short of a vigorous prosecution of the War, on our part, can now force the Mexican authorities to terms. For as you justly remark, we cannot now get out of the War with any degree of credit, except by large accessions of Territory, and such concessions will not be made by Mexico, but as a last resort to maintain her existence as a people. I should have rejoiced, if this War could have been avoided, but it is now, beyond our control, except by prosecuting it to a final issue.[41]

Even the Charleston *Mercury* with a new editor was disposed to insist on "a vigorous prosecution of the war, to the termination desired by all true patriots, of an honorable peace."[42] The *Southern Quarterly Review*, also published in Charleston, was still dubious about the effect "on the purity and excellence of our own institutions," if California and New Mexico were annexed to the United States.[43] No doubt slavery was one of the institutions which the Charleston journal had in mind. While there seems to have been a realization in the Southeast that more vigorous measures against Mexico were necessary, there was also an undercurrent of anxiety as to the probable result of those measures. The southerners were destined to become even more anxious as time went on.

But the demand for empire was growing apace in the West. The New Orleans *Picayune* asserted that the conquest of everything "north of the parallel of 22°," would not be "extravagant if it be pursued with a single view to extorting from Mexico such terms as it now befits the United States to exact. . . ."[44] According to the *Picayune*, the country had just begun to realize the "responsibility" of the Mexican

[40] Richmond *Enquirer*, 2 December 1846.
[41] *Correspondence Addressed to Calhoun*, p. 364.
[42] Charleston *Mercury*, 1 February 1847.
[43] *Southern Quarterly Review*, XI, 270.
[44] New Orleans *Picayune*, 7 October 1846.

War. The map of North America had "already taken a new aspect from the progress of our arms." There was no telling where the boundary would be located "if Mexico persists in the course which our last accounts show her determined to pursue."[45]   The stimulating effect of the acquisition of Mexican territory on the commerce of New Orleans was duly noted and recorded.[46]   Mexican intransigence might be beneficial after all. The Detroit *Free Press* insisted that it was nothing but right that Mexico should pay all the expenses of the war which "she so unwisely and so unjustly commenced."[47]   The Illinois *State Register* was sure that there was "but one opinion among the masses, in regard to the necessity of conquering Mexico." Whether the conquered territory would remain permanently a part of the United States could be determined later.[48]   If Illinois were to be allowed to make the decision there could be but little doubt that the conquered territory would remain a part of the United States.

It is obvious that if the Mexican War continued much longer demands for the annexation of the whole country would become numerous and strong. Some papers were already suggesting the Rio Grande and the thirtieth parallel of north latitude, the twenty-second parallel, and the Sierra Madre Mountains as a proper boundary between the United States and Mexico. Moreover, measures were recommended which if not directly designed to annihilate Mexican sovereignty could scarcely have had a different result. This campaign was ostensibly based on the fact that Mexican obstinacy had resulted in such an increase in the total expense of the war that the United States was justified in demanding more territory than Upper California and New Mexico. But the beckonings of manifest destiny and the commercial and industrial advantages to be derived from extensive annexations were not without influence on the expansionists.

---

[45] *Ibid.*, 11 October 1846.
[46] *De Bow's Review*, III, 107-108.
[47] Detroit *Free Press*, 22 December 1846.
[48] Illinois *State Register*, 5 February 1847.

Meanwhile, in December, 1846, Congress assembled for a session in which controversies regarding the Mexican War, territorial indemnity and slavery furnished practically the entire material for debate. Polk's message, presented to Congress on December 8, informed the legislators that temporary governments had been set up in California and New Mexico. While the war had " not been waged with a view to conquest," it would be prosecuted vigorously in order " to obtain an honorable peace, and thereby secure ample indemnity for the expenses of the war, as well as to our much injured citizens, who hold large pecuniary demands against Mexico." The President also repeated his request for a special appropriation to facilitate negotiations with Mexico.[49] These statements, together with a pronouncement from Senator Sevier, of Arkansas, which was considered as having been inspired by the administration, conveyed definite information to Congress that Upper California and New Mexico would be demanded from Mexico.[50]

In compliance with the President's request a bill providing three million dollars to meet any expenses which might be incurred in bringing the war to a close was introduced into Congress. Immediately the question of slavery was injected into the discussion. Throughout the session almost every Whig and Democrat in Congress expressed an opinion on the subject. All the Democrats seemed to be in favor of territorial acquisitions while the Whigs, generally speaking, were opposed. It appeared that some Democrats were disposed to demand more than Upper California and New Mexico. The principle of *uti possedetis* at the end of the war was suggested. It was intimated that the Sierra Madre Mountains would provide a more satisfactory boundary than the Rio Grande. Just at the end of the session the so-called Three Million Bill passed through both houses without the restrictions enunciated by the Wilmot Proviso.[51] The debates are interesting as showing the attitude of the parties and sections of the country

---

[49] *Cong. Globe, 29th Cong., 2d sess.*, p. 9.
[50] *Ibid.*, p. 306.   [51] *Ibid.*, p. 573.

on the acquisition of Mexican territory and whether that
territory should be slave or free.

As has been indicated the Whig party, North and South,
opposed the acquisition of territory from Mexico. Some
northern Whigs declared that they desired no territory under
any conditions.[52] Others, particularly in the Northeast, indicated their willingness to acquire territory on the Pacific
Ocean if it could be secured under the proper circumstances.[53]
All Whigs of the free states insisted that if any territory were
added to the United States it must not be open to slavery.
Southern Whigs were if anything more generally opposed to
the acquisition of Mexican territory than were their northern
colleagues. They were naturally enough, however, opposed
to the principles of the Wilmot Proviso. The resolutions of
Stephens, of Georgia, in the House, and Berrien, also of
Georgia, in the Senate, opposing the acquisition of territory,
fairly represented the attitude of slaveholding Whigs. The
position taken by the Whigs may be explained by their
partisan opposition to Democratic measures and by their fear
of the effect of the slavery issue on the fortunes of the Whig
party and the Union.[54]

Generally speaking the Democratic party looked with favor
on the acquisition of Upper California and New Mexico. The
majority of the members in both houses had not yet been
affected by the display of increased expansionist sentiment
which was appearing in the press. The question of slavery,
however, caused much strife in the ranks of the Democracy.
Northeastern Democrats insisted that any territory acquired
from Mexico must be free,[55] while Western Democrats were
so eager to get territory that they were willing not to press the

---

[52] For example, Hunt, Smith, Cilley, Webster and Davis, *ibid.*,
pp. 71-72, 124, 267, 422, 509.

[53] Darragh, of Pennsylvania, and Winthrop, of Massachusetts,
ibid., pp. 22, 146.

[54] For the attitude of the Southern Whigs, see Cole, *The Whig
Party in the South*, pp. 104-134. See also statements of Thomasson,
Toombs, Bell, Mangum, Berrien, Morehead and Stephens, *Cong.
Globe, 29th Cong., 2d sess.*, pp. 57, 142, 211, 309-310, 345, 401.

[55] See speeches of Dix, Wilmot, Dillingham and Niles, *ibid.*, pp.
334, 354, 402, 531-532.

slavery question until the territory was actually in the Union.[56] Opinions among southeastern Democrats were many and varied. Senators Westcott, of Florida, and Butler, of South Carolina, were alarmed at the slavery agitation and expressed themselves as being somewhat dubious about the desirability of acquiring any territory under the circumstances.[57] On the other hand Bagby, of Alabama, and Colquitt, of Georgia, exhibited no misgivings on the subject of slavery. There were both willing to take the territory and then face the consequences.[58] Calhoun was apparently not opposed to a moderate cession of Mexican territory, but he foresaw more clearly than anyone else the approach of the " irrepressible conflict." To meet the onslaughts of the anti-slavery forces the Carolinian advanced the doctrine that Congress could not exclude slavery from any of the territories of the United States.[59] Unless something could be done about the slavery issue, Democratic plans of expansion might be completely frustrated by strife within the party concerning the institutions which should prevail in the acquired territory.

In spite of party difficulties some Democratic congressmen appeared to be affected by the rising tide of expansionist sentiment. Representative Owen, of Indiana, was satisfied that if the war continued much longer public opinion would demand the cession of Lower California in addition to New Mexico and Upper California.[60] Parrish, of Ohio, " would go for acquiring in Mexico, as he had in Oregon, the greatest territory that could be honorably attained. . . . " [61] Senator Sevier, of Arkansas, Chairman of the Committee on Foreign Relations, " supposed that no Senator would think they ought to get less than New Mexico and Upper California. . . . " In the-course of his remarks, Sevier intimated that if the war continued more territory should be acquired from Mexico.[62]

---

[56] For sentiments of Sevier, Cass and Hannegan, see *ibid.*, pp. 306, 367-370, 515-517.   [59] *Ibid.*, pp. 356-357, 455.
    [57] *Ibid.*, pp. 409-410, 448.   [60] *Ibid.*, p. 109.
    [58] *Ibid.*, pp. 424, 439.   [61] *Ibid.*, p. 380.
    [62] *Ibid.*, p. 306; *Niles' Register*, LXXI, 372-373. Commenting on Sevier's remark, Senator Reverdy Johnson, a Whig of Maryland, said: " The terms on which they are to have peace still more oner-

Representative Tibbatts, of Kentucky, thought that the boundary between the United States and Mexico should be the Sierra Madre Mountains. But he would not take a "foot of land" beyond the Rio Grande without "just compensation" to Mexico.[63] In January, 1847, Representative Sims, of South Carolina, expressed sentiments suggesting the possibility of the acquisition of all Mexico.

> . . . we have a right to make conquests, to occupy the country, to establish provisional governments; and to seize upon even more than is necessary to indemnify us for the injuries we complain of and the expenses of the war. I have also attempted to show that, should it be necessary, we may rightfully and without any great danger, looking to an overruling Providence and to the patriotism of our people, permanently occupy this country. And I have no doubt—I express the opinion here—that every foot of territory we shall permanently occupy south of thirty-six degrees thirty minutes, will be slave territory.[64]

Giles, of Maryland, urged that the United States "march from Texas straight to the Pacific Ocean." It was the "destiny of the white race . . . the destiny of the Anglo-Saxon race." If the Anglo-Saxons failed to perform they would "not come up to that high position which Providence, in his mighty government, has assigned them." [65] Apparently some Democrats in Congress were prepared to aid in carrying out the design of the celestial powers. They had already begun to look toward the "Halls of the Montezumas" with covetous eyes.

The second session of the Twenty-ninth Congress revealed the fact that so far as Congress was concerned demands for Mexican territory had increased since the beginning of the war. At the close of the first session of the above Congress

---

ous! Why it will take the whole of Mexico, then (a Senator exclaimed: Precisely;) and they should hear from the opposite side of the Chamber what they had frequently heard from the Senator from Michigan [Cass] before—'The whole or none!'" *Cong. Globe,* *29th Cong., 2d sess.,* p. 336. Although Johnson apparently misquoted Sevier, the latter made no denial.

[63] *Ibid.,* p. 148. If the Wilmot Proviso should prevail, however, Tibbatts did not desire any territory at all.

[64] *Ibid.,* pp. 290-291. Sentiments of this character were seldom expressed by representatives from the Southeast.

[65] *Ibid.,* p. 387.

there was lack of a definite demand for any specific territory beyond the Rio Grande River. By March, 1847, however, it was known that at least Upper California and New Mexico must be ceded to the United States. The proposed acquisition of these territories met with general approval from the Democratic party. There were also indications that some members of Congress would not be satisfied with New Mexico and Upper California if the War did not soon come to an end. Demands for Lower California and the Sierra Madre Mountains as a boundary had already seen the light. If the war continued and the slavery argument did not become too ominous, additional territorial demands might be expected to appear in the national legislature.

Until the fall of 1847 the administration still held on to the original plans of territorial conquest, thus lagging behind the extreme expansionists. In September, 1846, however, Mexico had been warned that a prolongation of the war would render the conclusion of a satisfactory peace more difficult.[66] Buchanan suggested that the United States hold on to New Mexico and California and defend them. The Secretary of State did not desire any more territory but he thought that the United States ought to encourage the other northern provinces of Mexico to set up an independent government. Other cabinet members agreed with Buchanan.[67] The President, himself, thought that " New Mexico and California is all that can ever probably be acquired by Treaty, and indeed all that I think it important to acquire." [68] On April 15, 1847, Nicholas P. Trist was sent to Mexico to attempt to negotiate a peace. Trist was directed to attempt to secure New Mexico and both Californias, together with the right of transit across the Isthmus of Tehuantepec. For these concessions the United States would pay as much as thirty million dollars. " The extension of our boundaries over New Mexico and Upper California," Trist was instructed, " for a

[66] McCormac, pp. 446-447.
[67] Polk's *Diary*, II, 301; McCormac, pp. 464-465.
[68] Polk's *Diary*, II, 308; Buchanan to Donelson, 29 January 1847, Donelson MSS.

sum not exceeding twenty million dollars, is to be a sine qua non of any Treaty." The United States would also assume the payment of the claims of its citizens against Mexico.[69] Polk was later to rue the day when he sent Trist to Mexico. For it was this man who finally thwarted the President's plans of expansion and probably prevented the absorption of Mexico. But that happened almost a year later when the cession of Upper California and New Mexico no longer represented the minimum demands of the administration.

It was undoubtedly the slavery controversy which was partially responsible for the moderation of Polk, Buchanan and Walker.[70] In relation to the acquisition of any Mexican territory, and hence to the development of a sentiment for the absorption of all Mexico, the Wilmot Proviso reared its head as an obstacle to expansion which must be overcome before the expansionists could hope for success. Either for political reasons or on account of opposition to slavery, or both together, northern Whigs were already opposing the acquisition of territory with all their might. Their slaveholding allies followed suit with perhaps even more ardor, though for different reasons so far as slavery was concerned. The Wilmot Proviso tended to array northern Democrat against southern Democrat and thus divide the forces committed to expansion in the face of a Whig party united in its opposition to expansion though divided like the Democrats on the question of slavery.[71] The situation did not look promising to the advocates of empire in the early months of 1847.

---

[69] Buchanan to Trist, 15 April 1847, Trist MSS; McCormac, pp. 491-492.
[70] Polk's *Diary*, II, 308-309, 350.
[71] The Democratic party was already rent by internal divisions. The resentment of the Van Burenites has already been pointed out. The Oregon question caused more trouble within the ranks of the Democrats. Many western Democrats charged that they had been deserted by their southern allies in the matter of securing all Oregon. There is evidence that Senators Allen, of Ohio, and Hannegan, of Indiana, and Representative McDowell, of Ohio, among others, were highly displeased with the conduct of southern Democrats. *Cong. Globe, 29th Cong., 1st sess.*, pp. 110, 140; H. H. Leavitt to John McLean, 2 July 1846, McLean MSS. Some southerners admitted that the South had not acted in good faith. J. H. Lumpkin to

The expansionist press at the North realized that a program of expansion could scarcely be carried out by a divided Democracy against the Whig opposition. Accordingly representative newspapers of the North and Northwest opposed the introduction of the slavery issue in connection with territorial acquisitions. The Boston *Post* declared that " questions not necessarily involved in the voting of supplies should be excluded. When the war is over . . . the question of slave territory . . . can be entertained and discussed with the deliberation . . . [its] importance may require." [72] " The people think," said the New York *Herald*, " that it is time enough to talk about slavery in the new territory, after that new territory shall have been first ceded to us by Treaty, and regularly annexed to the United States." [73] The Illinois *State Register* was highly indignant at the continued slavery agitation. " The disorganizing spirit of abolitionism," said the editor, " pandered to by the Whig party, has interposed its blighting influence at a crisis when the honor of the nation and the credit of our arms are at stake." [74] Other papers took up the cry, not because they were friendly to slavery but because they were afraid that the creation of a sectional issue would prevent the acquisition of any territory.[75]

And the fears of the expansionists seem to have been justified to some extent for in both North and South the slavery

---

Howell Cobb, 13 November 1846, Ulrich B. Phillips, ed., *The Correspondence of Robert Toombs, Alexander H. Stephens, and Howell Cobb*, in *Annual Report of the American Historical Association for 1911*, II, 86. If the slavery question were to be allowed to further divide the Democrats then much of the party strength would be dissipated and Democratic plans of empire wrecked.

[72] Boston *Post*, 21 January 1847.

[73] New York *Herald*, 11 January 1847.

[74] Illinois *State Register*, 29 January 1847.

[75] *Democratic Review*, XX, 102; Detroit *Free Press*, 22 March 1847; Albany *Argus*, quoted by *Niles' Register*, LXXIII, 45; Philadelphia *Ledger*, quoted by Nashville *Union*, 6 October 1847. The most widely read paper in Illinois declared: " We are aware that a majority of the people of Illinois are opposed to the extension of slavery in the territory we may acquire from Mexico; but we deny that they are in favor of weighing down the war measures of the government with collateral questions, and exciting sectional issues." Illinois *State Register*, 26 March 1847.

controversy tended to check the growth of expansionist sentiment. Lewis Cass and James Buchanan, both angling for
the support of the Democracy in the next presidential campaign, were convinced that public opinion at the North
would not support the acquisition of Mexican territory south
of the Missouri Compromise line or at least south of the
thirty-second parallel, since it was thought that such territory
would be suitable for slavery.[76] Northern and southern
Whigs, with more or less sincerity, demanded that no territory whatever be taken from Mexico as annexations in that
quarter would threaten the existence of the Union.[77] As has
already been noted, such southern Democratic leaders in Congress as Calhoun, Butler, Wescott and Tibbatts looked with
disfavor on extensive territorial conquests under existing conditions. Other southern Democrats expressed their disapproval of the dismemberment of Mexico. Among them were
Thomas Cobb, of Georgia, Joel R. Poinsett, of South Carolina,
and Joseph W. Lesesne, of Alabama.[78] It is true that some
southern newspapers insisted that territory be acquired and
that the South stand up for its rights in that territory.[79]
Other organs, however, thought that it might be better to
forego any further expansion if the slavery question could
not be satisfactorily settled. Said the Charleston *Mercury*:

---

[76] Buchanan to Shields, 23 April 1847, Buchanan's *Works*, VII,
286-287; Jefferson Davis to Stephen Cocke, 30 November 1847,
Dunbar Rowland, ed., *Jefferson Davis, Constitutionalist, His Letters, Papers and Speeches*, I, 180-181. Cass had apparently explained
to Davis his reasons for caution in the spring of 1847.

[77] For the northern Whig viewpoint, see a speech of Thomas Cor-
win at Lebanon, Ohio, August 28, 1847, *Niles' Register*, LXXIII,
44, and the remarks of Representative Smith, of Indiana, *Cong.
Globe, 29th Cong., 2d sess.*, p. 124. For the southern Whigs, see
Cole, pp. 121-122; Richmond *Whig*, quoted by *Niles' Register*,
LXXIII, 47.

[78] Thomas Cobb to Howell Cobb, 23 June 1847, *Toombs, Stephens,
Cobb Correspondence*, p. 88; Poinsett to Van Buren, 4 June 1847,
Van Buren MSS; Lesesne to Calhoun, 24 August 1847, J. Franklin
Jameson, ed., *Correspondence of John C. Calhoun*, in *Annual Report
of the American Historical Association for 1899*, II, 1130.

[79] Richmond *Enquirer*, 20 January 1847; Augusta *Constitutionalist*, quoted in *ibid.*; New Orleans *Commercial Times* quoted in *ibid.*,
24 February 1847.

The waters of bitterness have flowed too long, and distrust of the North is too fully awakened, to allow much chance for reconciliation now. Mexican wars and California acquisitions—600,000 square miles, all told of craggy mountains and desert plains,—are of little moment to the Southern States compared with the maintenance of their just rights in the Union. They will not sell the latter for the former.[80]

There was little chance for the development of a strong sentiment for extensive annexations of Mexican territory while the Wilmot Proviso remained to plague the Democratic party.

While the period from October, 1846, to March, 1847, witnessed the appearance of an increased expansionist sentiment in the United States, there also developed a bitter controversy on the status of slavery in any territory which might be acquired from Mexico. The one force tended to counteract the other and it was a doubtful question as to which would prove more potent in the end. Beginning in March, 1847, however, there were indications that the expansionists might ultimately be able to override all obstructions in their path. General Taylor's victory at Buena Vista and Scott's achievements around Vera Cruz fired the imagination of the American people. As time went on the lust for conquest increased and the public demanded ever more drastic treatment of Mexico. Expressions of belief that the war could end only with the absorption of all Mexico became more numerous. When it was seen that Trist was making little headway in his negotiations, the administration began to lean toward more severe terms of peace. In the meantime the slavery question began to take on new aspects. There could be noted the emergence of a feeling that Mexican territory was not suitable for the existence of slavery. This tended to cause the removal of the issue presented by the Wilmot Proviso. While many southerners continued their opposition to expansion, the northern Democracy no longer insisted on the Wilmot Proviso with so much vehemence. Much of its force as a disturbing factor in the party was lost. The slavery issue

---

[80] Charleston *Mercury*, 15 February 1847. For like expressions, see *Southern Quarterly Review*, XII, 94; "Publicola," *Southern Literary Messenger*, XIII, 431.

remained but not in such form that it would be likely to rend the Democratic party asunder before Mexico could be dismembered. This third phase in the development of the sentiment for all Mexico may be said to have begun about March or April, 1847, and to have ended in October of the same year.

News of the success of the American armies in Mexico brought forth both prophecies and suggestions from eastern expansionist circles. The victories of Taylor and Scott convinced the editor of the Boston *Post* that " this ' miserable war ' will do more for the spread of commercial and political freedom, the prosperity and glory of the United States, than any event since the declaration of American Independence." [81] Some months later an article in the same paper pointed out one way in which the happy results pictured by the editor might be accomplished. "We can," said the writer, "and may be obliged to, overrun and conquer Mexico; but the conquest of a nation is not the work of a single hour, day, month or year." [82] Shortly after the departure of Trist for Mexico, New York papers undertook to give advice as to how the Mexican problem might be settled. The *Democratic Review* contended that " no faith can be reposed in such a people " as the Mexicans. The proper procedure would be " a twenty years occupation of the chief cities at their expense, as hostages for peace." However desirable peace might be, there was no safety " in trusting a divided nation, the reasonable part of which has no power to fulfill its negotiations, and the remainder no disposition to recognize the engagements of those in power." [83] The *Herald* suggested similar measures. A military government should be established in Mexico, and direct taxes collected from the people and the church. This would support " whatever forces may be necessary to keep the country in subjection." The United States should "hold on, if necessary, to the crack of doom." " The universal Yankee nation," continued the *Herald*, " can regenerate and

[81] Boston *Post*, 5 April 1847.
[82] " John Smith, Jr.," in *ibid.*, 10 August 1847.
[83] *Democratic Review*, XX, 455.

disenthrall the people of Mexico in a few years; and we believe it is a part of our destiny to civilize that beautiful country, and enable its inhabitants to appreciate some of the many advantages and blessings they enjoy." [84] There was nothing to prevent the Yankees, also, from enjoying some of the many advantages and blessings which Mexico afforded.

As the summer advanced expressions from New York became more thoroughgoing. A New York Democrat, expressing his disapproval of the annexation of Mexico, declared: " But *now* we must take her, in order to keep her from the hands of others. . . . We have started upon the course of conquest, we cannot now recede if we would, our success will create circumstances to impel us onward in that direction, whether we are willing or not." [85] In August, the *Herald* declared that if the Mexicans did not take advantage of Trist's offers and agree to a peace, " Mexico will most assuredly lose her nationality." [86] The *Democratic Review* felt it necessary to issue a word of warning:

The annexation of the country to the United States would be a calamity. 5,000,000 ignorant and indolent half-civilized Indians, with 1,500,000 free negroes and mulattoes, the remnants of the British slave trade, would scarcely be a desirable incumbrance, even with the great natural wealth of Mexico.[87]

To many citizens of the United States, however, the " great natural wealth " of Mexico was worth almost any burden which its possession might involve.

Farther South, the same forces were at work. In May, one of Calhoun's correspondents wrote from Washington: " This nation is infatuated with victory and conquest. . . ." The writer thought that the war with Mexico would " end in annexing the whole country." [88] The obstinacy of the Mexi-

---

[84] New York *Herald*, 15 May 1847.
[85] Byrdsall to Calhoun, 19 July 1847, *Correspondence of Calhoun*, p. 1127. Before the war Byrdsall had demanded the annexation of all Mexico. See above, p. 27n. He was either not sincere in his disapproval, or else, following Calhoun, had begun to fear the issue of slavery.
[86] New York *Herald*, 10 August 1847.
[87] *Democratic Review*, XXI, 101.
[88] N. Towson to Calhoun, 27 May 1847, *Correspondence Addressed to Calhoun*, pp. 379-380.

cans aroused the ire of the *National Whig*, a Taylor organ at the national capital. The editor asserted that the United States "must conquer, occupy and make the enemy pay the cost by seizing upon all private and corporate property, including the property of the church, which is valued at one hundred and fifty millions of dollars." [89] This certainly would be "conquering a peace" with a vengeance and incidentally everything else which was worth conquering. The *National Whig*, naturally enough, did not deem it necessary to mention the property which under this plan would be left to Mexico and the Mexicans. The *National Era*, an anti-slavery journal, also published at Washington, announced to the public that thus far the extension of territory had "strengthened the bonds of union." "Mexico and the United States," continued the editorial, "constitute *one geographical system*, all the parts of which may be easily made accessible to each other . . . [and] if under one political system, would possess a remarkable community of interests." Coming directly to the point, the editor concluded:

The annexation of the Mexican States on the plan proposed, always, of course, *with their own free will and consent*, would complete our continental boundaries South, secure a basis of 4,000,000 square miles for our empire, establish Freedom as the fundamental and unchangeable Law of the North American continent, and give Republicanism the perpetual ascendancy over all other forms of government. [90]

The *National Era* probably knew that it would be easy enough for the United States army in Mexico to hold a "free" plebiscite which would record the willingness of the Mexicans to come into the Union. Were the anti-slavery forces about to begin the march to Mexico City? One wonders what the champions of the "pro-slavery conspiracy" theory thought when they read the above editorial. Whatever the thought they apparently kept it to themselves.

Although there seemed to be more resistance to the lure of conquest south of Washington, even here—in the bailiwick of

---

[89] *National Whig*, 17 May 1847, quoted by the New Orleans *Picayune*, 26 May 1847.
[90] *National Era*, 19 August 1847.

Calhoun — military glory stirred the emotions. As early as April 12, an article in the Charleston *Mercury* predicted that "what Cortez effected with 500 men may be accomplished with the combined armies of Scott and Taylor, exceeding 16,000 soldiers; and all fresh from the victories they have so recently achieved." Readers were asked to recall this prediction "when conquered Mexico submits or sues for annexation." [91] The *Mercury*, whose editor had at one time advised the United States forces to stop at the Rio Grande, now advocated the Sierra Madre Mountains as the boundary prescribed by nature between the two countries.[92] "The national pride has become inflamed," said a southern clergyman, "the passion for acquisition has been indulged by way of contemplation. . . ." [93] Calhoun thought that if the United States continued victorious "it would seem impossible almost to stop short of the Conquest of the country." [94] An Alabama supporter of Calhoun wrote in August that there was "at the South a large party in favor of the acquisition of territory." The "insane thirst" for territory, according to the writer, was the "great American disease." [95]

The likelihood of extensive territorial conquests brought forth doleful comments from southern leaders. To annex Mexico, said Calhoun, "would be to overthrow our government, and, to hold it as a Province, to corrupt and destroy it." [96] It would mean in all probability that the army and navy would be the "controlling influence" in the United States for at least a generation.[97] According to Poinsett, another South Carolinian, the acquisition of any Mexican territory would "embroil us in domestic squabbles interminable and most dangerous. . . ." [98] To avoid these squabbles

---

[91] "One who Predicted," Charleston *Mercury*, 12 April 1847.
[92] *Ibid.*, 19 June 1847.
[93] J. N. Danforth, *Southern Literary Messenger*, XXIII, 502.
[94] Calhoun to Clemson, 15 June 1847, *Correspondence of Calhoun*, p. 734.
[95] Lesesne to Calhoun, 24 August 1847, *ibid.*, p. 1130.
[96] Calhoun to Clemson, 15 June 1847, *ibid.*, p. 734.
[97] Calhoun to Mrs. Clemson, 10 June 1847, *ibid.*, p. 731.
[98] Poinsett to Van Buren, 4 June 1847, Van Buren MSS.

Lesesne told of " a growing disposition among our friends to come out boldly against the further acquisition of Territory as the only practicable mode of saving the south against the danger that threatens from this alarming question [Wilmot Proviso]." [99]   It apparently required courage to attempt to cure the " great American disease." Robert Toombs, voicing sentiments common to southern Whigs, declared:

> I begin to fear that the question is fast approaching a crisis.   It seems our successes in Mexico have greatly raised the pretensions of Polk and his cabinett [sic] and the weakness and divisions of Mexico will in all probability induce her to accede to terms . . . which will be disgracefull to her and ruinous to us.   You are aware of my early and uniform disrelish of the idea of the appropriation of Mexican Territory.   I can see nothing but evil to come of it.   And now I do not clearly see how it can be avoided to some extent.[100]

It seems that many southerners thought that the trend of events indicated the acquisition of large amounts of Mexican territory, perhaps the whole of Mexico.   Since it was believed that this would lead to a fierce sectional struggle concerning the " peculiar institution," the prospect of extensive annexations was viewed with alarm by influential southerners of both political parties.

The West contributed its share to the rapidly mounting tide of expansionist sentiment.   Speaking of the supposed English mediation, the Illinois *State Register* declared: " We have right and power on our side, and there is no cause for irresolution.   We can take as much Mexican territory as we may want, and no power dare oppose it except by paper bullet protests." [101]   When it appeared that Trist would not likely be able to arrange terms of peace, the Detroit *Free Press* expressed characteristic western sentiments:

> Now that the letter of Mr. Buchanan has been acted upon by the authorities in Mexico, the administration of the United States know on what ground they stand and what is to be done.   The ' olive branch ' has been extended, but the late action of the Mexican Con-

---

[99] Lesesne to Calhoun, 24 August 1847, *Correspondence of Calhoun*, p. 1130.

[100] Toombs to Calhoun, 30 April 1847, *Correspondence Addressed to Calhoun*, p. 373.   For a similar expression, see Richmond *Whig*, quoted by *Niles' Register*, LXXIII, 47.

[101] Illinois *State Register*, 22 April 1847.

gress is the first authoritative rejection of peace offers since the commencement of the war. It will not be rejected again, for want of opportunity. Ere this, dispatches are on the way to the army to move on, we cannot doubt. All that remains to be done is to call out 20, or 40,000 more volunteers.[102]

From Louisiana came the statement that the " opinion is becoming more and more general that the United States may conquer Mexico; but a peace—never." [103] While there was no definite pronouncement as to the ultimate fate of Mexico, she could scarcely expect moderation from the West if the day of judgment were long delayed.

As the fall of 1847 approached and there was still no definite results from Trist's mission, Polk and his cabinet became converted to the idea of more drastic terms of peace.[104] On September 4, the President declared that if the war continued he would not be prepared to pay the sum for California and New Mexico which Trist had been authorized to offer in April. A few days later Polk asked the cabinet to consider the question as to whether or not the amount of territory to be demanded from Mexico should be increased and the money payment decreased. It was agreed at once that Mexico should be offered less money for whatever cessions were made. Buchanan suggested that the parallel of thirty-one degrees or thirty-one degrees thirty minutes should be the boundary from the Rio Grande to the Gulf of California, instead of thirty-two degrees as provided in Trist's instructions. Walker and Clifford were in favor of acquiring

---

[102] Detroit *Free Press*, 25 August 1847.

[103] New Orleans *Picayune*, 19 May 1847.

[104] In May, George Bancroft, American minister to Great Britain, wrote Polk: " I am able to-day to announce to you a very great and decided change in the views of England with reference to our war with Mexico. . . . England is even preparing to hear of our negotiating for half, or two thirds, or even the whole of Mexico. . . ." *Life and Letters of George Bancroft*, II, 17-18. A few days later, Bancroft also wrote Buchanan that while England did not like to see the territory of the United States increase, she saw "the inevitable necessity which appropriates all North America to the Anglo-Saxon Race." Buchanan's *Works*, VII, 309. These letters were suggestive at any rate and showed that apparently no overt opposition was to be expected from Great Britain however much of Mexico the United States should attempt to annex.

Tamaulipas, including the port of Tampico.   The other cabinet members were opposed to this increase of territory. Polk was desirous of securing Tamaulipas if practicable, but expressed his approval of Buchanan's proposal.   It was agreed to await further news from Mexico before taking definite action.[105]   Slowly but surely the administration was preparing to demand another slice of Mexican territory.

The sentiment not only of the administration but also of the entire country would be powerfully affected by the receipt of unfavorable reports from Mexico.   The belief was becoming widespread that the war could only be ended by the conquest of the whole country and long continued occupation by United States troops.   Not many were as yet ready to recommend openly annexation in any form, but proposals for conquest and occupation, if carried out, could scarcely have had a different result.   Moreover, one of the leading anti-slavery journals in the United States looked with approval on the annexation of all Mexico if it were accomplished with the consent of the Mexicans.   In short, it might be said that increasing numbers of people in the United States were becoming familiar with the idea that the war might end in a permanent connection between Mexico and the United States. To many this would be a desirable consummation of events, and should Mexico continue to refuse an acceptable peace the expansionists could be expected to express themselves in more concrete terms.

The great obstruction which had hitherto prevented the expansionist forces from developing to their full strength was, of course, the sectional controversy over slavery.   But by the fall of 1847 the way had been prepared for minimizing the effect of this issue on the expansionist movement.   As we have seen, northern expansionists had been fighting the Wilmot Proviso on the grounds that it would prevent the acquisition of any Mexican territory.   Was there not some means by which the slavery issue could be sidetracked until

---

[105] Polk's *Diary*, III, 161-165; McCormac, pp. .517-518; Edward G. Bourne, " The United States and Mexico, 1847-1848," *American Historical Review*, V, 493-494.

Mexico had made the desired cessions of territory? If the northern Democracy could be persuaded to waive the question, at least for the time, the threatened breach in the Democratic party might be closed. But how was such a feat to be accomplished? Could it not be shown that the Wilmot Proviso was not needed to prevent the introduction of slavery into territory taken from Mexico? This line of reasoning must have exerted considerable influence at the North, for from the first appearance of the question as a serious problem there appeared evidences of a sustained attempt to show the opponents of slavery that their fears of its extension were groundless.

Even before the annexation of Texas there could be heard voices here and there which proclaimed that the anti-slavery forces had nothing to fear from expansion at the expense of Mexico. These pronouncements came in connection with discussions on annexation. While the question was still pending, General Thomas J. Green, a prominent Texan, expressed himself on the subject. While Green was an ardent supporter of slavery and made no apologies for the institution, he confessed that the day would probably come within a generation when " either from individual interest or public policy, the white and black man can no longer occupy the same soil." The General undertook to show that by annexing Texas and other portions of Mexico there would be secured an ideal location for establishing the presumably freed blacks when it became necessary to remove them from the settled portions of the United States.[106] It may be contended that Green was merely trying to reconcile the anti-slavery element in the United States to the idea of expansion. This is probably true enough. Yet at the same time there was advanced a similar argument in the Congress of the United States by a member from a free state. Discussing the effect of the annexation of Texas, Robert Dale Owen, of Indiana, informed the House of Representatives on January 8, 1845, that expansion would tend to remove large numbers of slaves from .

---

[106] Green, *Journal of the Texian Expedition against Mier*, pp. 412, 418, 433.

the border states and aid in effecting " peaceful and gradual emancipation " in all the states.[107] W. T. Sherman, who certainly did not support the extension of slavery and therefore cannot be accused of insincerity, was convinced that the annexation of Texas would prove injurious to the interests of slaveholders.[108] If that were true, further expansion would be even more disastrous in its effects on the slavocracy.

But the views expressed by such men as Green, Owen and Sherman did not find general acceptance in the United States. On the contrary, one may assert with a reasonable degree of assurance that an overwhelming majority of people who had any opinion on the subject thought that southwestward expansion meant an increase in the strength of slavery and slaveholders. Therefore, when Wilmot introduced his firebrand into Congress, the issue presented seemed to be a real one. A perusal of contemporary newspapers, debates in Congress and private correspondence reveals the earnestness and sincerity of most of the disputants of 1846. Hence the necessity from the expansionist viewpoint of removing, if possible, the Wilmot Proviso from the realm of current politics.

The contentions of most of those who opposed Wilmot's proposition at the North were based on the assumption that any territory taken from Mexico would be free, or at least that such annexations would tend to weaken slavery. There were some, however, who contended that from a legal point of view Congress was merely wasting time arguing about slavery. Thus John Quincy Adams asserted that slavery could only be established in territory conquered from Mexico by the treaty of cession. He would, therefore, not insist that Congress sanction the proposal of Wilmot, although it met with his approval.[109] The anti-slavery *National Era* contended that the United States government did not have " constitutional

---

[107] *Cong. Globe, 28th Cong., 2d sess.*, p. 111.
[108] W. T. Sherman to John Sherman, 29 August 1845, Rachel S. Thorndike, ed., *The Sherman Letters: Correspondence between General and Senator Sherman from 1837 to 1891*, p. 28.
[109] *Cong. Globe, 29th Cong., 1st sess.*, p. 1216.

power to establish slavery in the free territory acquired from Mexico." [110] Much the same idea was advanced by Judge McLean, of Ohio, when he announced that neither Congress nor the treaty-making authorities could introduce the South's peculiar institution into the proposed territorial conquests.[111] Robert Dale Owen was convinced that slavery must be imposed on California by positive law or it would not exist there at all. "And if so," said he, "no Missouri Compromise is necessary to exclude it from territories north of thirty-six and a half, nor any Wilmot Proviso to shut it out south of that parallel." [112] From these statements, most, though not all, coming from expansionists, it is obvious that the anti-slavery northerner was supposed to conclude that he need not be greatly concerned about the fate of the Wilmot Proviso.

But it does not appear that arguments based on legal considerations had very much effect on northern public opinion. It was doubtless recognized that mere illegality might not be a sufficient deterrent to the spread of slavery. Moreover, the question of the power or the lack of power of Congress in the premises was by no means settled. Leading men at the South were beginning to meet their northern opponents with assertions that neither Congress, nor a territorial legislature, nor even the inhabitants of the territory had any right to prohibit or abolish slavery in the territories of the United States.[113] If the southerners were correct there was no legal method of preventing the advance of slavery into the territories. From the anti-slavery point of view southern claims should not be allowed to go unchallenged. All the more reason for joining battle in favor of the Wilmot Proviso. Having failed to make out a convincing case for removing the slavery question from the halls of Congress on legal grounds, northern propagandists then endeavored to show

---

[110] *National Era*, 14 January 1847.

[111] Detroit *Free Press*, 17 January 1848. McClean was an associate justice of the Supreme Court and a Whig aspirant for the Presidency.

[112] Robert Dale Owen, "Slavery Extension Question," Princeton *Clarion*, copy dated September 9, 1847 in Van Buren MSS.

[113] For opinions of Calhoun, Bagby and Yulee, see *Cong. Globe, 29th Cong., 2d sess.*, p. 455; *ibid., 30th Cong., 1st sess.*, pp. 261, 350.

that on account of natural conditions, and without any legal restrictions as to slavery, expansion toward the Southwest could not benefit slaveholders.

Arguments used to prove the point were many and various. It was maintained in some quarters that slavery for economic reasons was slowly passing away from its accustomed haunts. The annexation of Mexican territory could only serve to hasten the process. The *New Englander*, extremely hostile to slavery, insisted that there were signs which indicated that slavery in the South was not to be a permanent institution. Rapid expansion of cotton production would soon overtake the demand and then the economic basis of slavery would be undermined. Coming directly to the point, the editor declared:

no matter what new domains may be acquired by conquest or by any other process of annexation, for the extension of slavery—no matter what new markets for human cattle may be opened beyond the Rio Grande or upon the shores of the Pacific—the value of slave labor, and therefore of slaves, will be diminished, and that which has so long been the sustenance and growth of slavery will be taken away.[114]

Thomas George, in a published article, called on the opponents of slavery to cease lending their support to the Wilmot Proviso which was not only unconstitutional but if adopted would be fatal to the chief end of the anti-slavery cohorts. George argued that slaves were steadily retreating southward. In a few years Virginia and some other states would be free. " But close the avenues of egress, and the effect will be like that produced by checking the perspiration of the human body;—the humors will remain in the system—its vital action will be deranged, and a miserable dissolution will ensue." [115] One of the leading expansionist organs at the North took up the cudgels in defense of the same theory.[116] From other sources came like statements.[117] In other words,

---

[114] *New Englander*, V, 317-318.
[115] " Sectional Rights under the Constitution," *Democratic Review*, XXI, 103-106.
[116] New York *Herald*, 17 October 1847.
[117] For examples, see letter of Foster Hooper, Democratic candidate for Congress from Massachusetts, Boston *Post*, 4 November 1846; H. B. Aulting to Donelson, 29 March 1847, Donelson MSS;

it would behoove the defenders of the Wilmot Proviso to surrender immediately since victory in 1847 really meant defeat
for their ultimate purpose.

Those who did not desire to see any increase in the area
of slavery, regardless of the ultimate effects on the institution, were not neglected in the campaign of public education.
For their benefit there was supplied an abundance of propaganda to prove that slavery would never be established in
any territory which Mexico might cede to the United States.
Representative papers like the New York *Herald,* the Philadelphia *Ledger,* the Boston *Post,* the Illinois *State Register,*
the St. Louis *Reveille* and the *National Era* joined the
chorus.[118] One powerful organ of public opinion admitted that
slavery might be introduced into the territory in question
" but from the very nature of things " contended that it was
" very improbable that a single slave would ever be trans-
ported there, were the North even willing to countenance
it." [119] There was no doubt at all about the matter in the
mind of another editor who asserted that " free labor must,
from necessity, occupy California and New Mexico." Slavery
could not " live along side of it, restriction or no restriction. . . ." [120] Other stories had it that California and the
rest of New Mexico already contained a population intensely
hostile to slavery and a multitude of Indians whose labor
was cheaper than that of the blacks. It was also maintained
that Mexican soil was not suited to slave labor.[121] If the
public mind should become sufficiently accustomed to such
ideas, the Wilmot Proviso could be very easily brushed aside.

Northern propagandists had allies at the South, for many
southerners, both Democrats and Whigs, joined the ranks

Byrdsall to Calhoun, 12 November 1847, *Correspondence Addressed
to Calhoun,* p. 410.
 [118] New York *Herald,* 11, 20 January 1847; Boston *Post,* 15 February 1847; Philadelphia *Ledger,* quoted by the Nashville *Union,* 6
October 1847; Illinois *State Register,* 8 October, 26 November 1847;
St. Louis *Reveille,* quoted in *ibid.,* 26 November 1847; *National Era,*
3 February 1848.
 [119] New York *Herald,* 20 January 1847.
 [120] Boston *Post,* 15 February 1847.
 [121] St. Louis *Reveille,* quoted by the Illinois *State Register,* 26
November 1847; *National Era,* 3 February 1848.

of those who said that slavery could not enter Mexican territory. Among the Democrats, President Polk and A. J. Donelson took that attitude.[122]   John A. Campbell concluded that Mexican territory was " wholly unfit for a negro population " and would probably enter the Union without slavery. Even if he were in error on this point, Campbell thought that the non-slaveholding states would be the largest beneficiaries.[123]   " Publicola," writing from Mississippi, suggested that the western territories might serve as an outlet " through which the race of slaves will ultimately disappear from the continent." [124]   For the Whigs, Senator Berrien, of Georgia, and Waddy Thompson, of South Carolina, asserted that no slaveholding states could be formed west of the Rio Grande.[125] Thompson was considered quite an authority on things Mexican. Consequently many people listened when he said: " I do not express an opinion lightly formed, but one upon which I would stake my existence, that, whether the principle of the Wilmot Proviso be enacted by Congress or not, slavery never will exist in any state which may be hereafter formed west of the Rio Grande." [126]   The Richmond *Whig* expressed a like opinion.[127]   For the most part southern propaganda was designed to build up an opinion at the South opposed to the acquisition of territory. But the arguments were rebroadcast by northern expansionists with a directly opposite purpose, that is, to create a sentiment at the North which would support expansion without insisting on the principles of the Wilmot Proviso.

From other quarters, however, especially among northern Whigs, there continued a vigorous support of the Wilmot Proviso and a sustained opposition to the war on the grounds that it was designed to extend slavery. To overcome the effect of this opposition the expansionists charged the Whigs

---

[122] Smith, I, 188; McCormac, pp. 618-619.
[123] Campbell to Calhoun, 20 November 1847, *Correspondence of Calhoun*, pp. 1140-1142.
[124] *Southern Literary Messenger*, XIII, 431.
[125] *Cong. Globe, 29th Cong., 2d sess.*, p. 330; Boston *Post*, 19 November 1847.
[126] Boston *Post*, 19 November 1847.
[127] Quoted in *ibid.*

and other supporters of the Wilmot Proviso with partisanship, insincerity and trickery. Said the Boston *Post*:

The cant about slavery in the territory *to be acquired* is not sincere. Mr. Berrien, senator from a slave state, offered a resolution in the U. S. Senate against the acquisition of any territory from Mexico, *because he was satisfied slavery never could exist in any such territory*. Mr. Johnson, another senator from a slave state, sustained Mr. Berrien's proposition, *because*, he said, *every foot of territory acquired from Mexico must INEVITABLY be free territory*. Therefore we believe that the Wilmot Proviso was not intended to guard the interests (: the free states, or to sustain the principle of freedom; but to throw a firebrand into the national councils—to aid political tricksters to form sectional parties.[128]

The Detroit *Free Press* branded as false the statement that the Whigs were opposed to territory only because it might be open to slavery. In support of his contention the editor reminded his public that northern and western Whigs had also opposed the acquisition of the Oregon territory which admittedly would have been free.[129] At least one southern newspaper took the same view. The editor of the New Orleans *Picayune* thought that there was nothing to " command fear or respect " about the Wilmot Proviso. The advocates of the Proviso did not want any territory and therefore they had injected the slavery issue into Congressional discussions in order to prevent expansion.[130] If the propagandists were to be believed, then, the advocates of Wilmot's Proviso were really not afraid of the extension of slavery but were using that bogey to prevent the acquisition of territory.

The results of this campaign of enlightenment became noticeable when, toward the close of 1847, leading Democratic politicians at the North joined in the clamor against the Wilmot Proviso. The presidential campaign of 1848 was approaching and it was necessary that would-be candidates make some sort of a statement, if possible, which would not tear down their political fences. Secretary of State, James Buchanan, and Senator Lewis Cass both denounced the slavery agitation but were careful to point out that economic

[128] Boston *Post*, 13 March 1847.
[129] Detroit *Free Press*, 22 March 1847.
[130] New Orleans *Picayune*, 14 January 1848.

conditions did not point to the existence of slavery in Mexican territory. As a concession to the South the principles of the Missouri Compromise or of " popular sovereignty " were suggested as means of solution for the slavery question.[131] In a speech at Pittsburgh in September, concerning slavery and the Wilmot Proviso, Vice-President Dallas declared:

> The very best thing which can be done, when all is said upon the subject that may be said, will be to let it alone entirely—*leaving to the people of the territory to be acquired the business of settling the matter for themselves*; for where slavery has no existence, all the legislation of Congress would be powerless to give it existence; and where we find it to exist, the people of the country have themselves adopted the institution; *they have the right alone to determine their own institutions,* and as the matter so exists elsewhere, they are not to be condemned for its existence.[132]

Thus to Dallas goes the credit or discredit, depending on the point of view, of having been one of the first to propose the doctrine of " popular " or " squatter sovereignty," later taken up by Cass, Douglas and others.[133] By condemning the Wilmot Proviso and supporting " popular sovereignty " the Vice-President was indirectly advising northern Democrats to cease their agitation and leave the question to the people of the territory who would themselves exclude slavery. To the same effect was a toast of Secretary of the Treasury, Robert J. Walker, at a Washington gathering in January, 1848:

> No state by legislation, past or prospective, nor Congress, by resolutions and enactments, direct or declatory, can force the peculiar local institutions of any state, north or south, into such Territories [annexed or conquered] against the will of their people, in violation of prior existing laws, and the fundamental principle of self-government.[134]

It was a recognition of the fact that " popular sovereignty " meant free territory which induced southerners to declare that

---

[131] A letter from Buchanan to a group of Pennsylvania Democrats is printed in the Richmond *Enquirer*, 3 September 1847. For a letter from Cass to A. O. P. Nicholson, dated December 29, 1847, see *Niles' Register*, LXXIII, 293.

[132] Richmond *Enquirer*, 29 September 1847. Italics in the *Enquirer*.

[133] As early as January 8, 1847, Representative Ligon, a Democrat of Maryland, proposed to allow the people of the territory concerned to decide the slavery question for themselves. *Cong. Globe, 29th Cong., 2d sess.*, p. 151.

[134] Detroit *Free Press*, 31 January 1848.

Congress must protect their property in the territories and that neither the people nor a territorial legislature could banish slavery. It is safe to assume that neither Cass, Buchanan, Dallas nor Walker had any idea that the adoption of the Missouri Compromise line or of " popular sovereignty " would result in an increase in the area of slavery. When politicians of this stripe were ready to publicly propose giving up the attempt to keep slavery out of territorial conquests by an act of Congress, one may be sure that in their opinion large numbers of Democratic voters at the North were in sympathy with their views. And to a certain extent the opinion was correct.[135]

At the South some men along with Jefferson Davis appeared highly gratified at the prospect of the elimination of the Wilmot Proviso.[136] Others did not think that the South was in any better position as regards slavery than before. John A. Campbell was convinced that Mexican territory would be free anyhow and for that reason he was opposed to territorial acquisitions under any conditions.[137] The Charleston *Mercury* contended that in effect the doctrine of Cass was no different from that of Wilmot. The latter desired that Congress should prevent slave property from going to the territory while the former suggested that " the people of the new territory shall be supported in refusing permission to the slaveholder to locate there." [138] Where

---

[135] For instance the legislature of New Hampshire, which had endorsed the Wilmot Proviso earlier in 1847, passed resolutions later opposing any legislation by Congress on the subject. *Niles' Register*, LXXIII, 44; *Cong. Globe, 30th Cong., 1st sess.*, p. 51. The Indiana legislature and Democratic conventions in Ohio and Indiana also expressed disapproval of the Wilmot Proviso. One observer noted that the " disposition to escape from the Wilmot Proviso is becoming general among the politicians and people, not the abolitionists or Eastern folks." H. W. Conner to Calhoun, 6 October 1847, *Correspondence Addressed to Calhoun*, pp. 402-403; Elwood Fisher to Calhoun, 17 January 1848, *ibid.*, p. 423; Detroit *Free Press*, 31 January 1848.

[136] Davis to Cocke, 30 November 1847, Rowland, *Jefferson Davis*, I, 180-181.

[137] Campbell to Calhoun, 20 November 1847, *Correspondence of Calhoun*, pp. 1140-1142.

[138] Charleston *Mercury*, 17 January 1848.

such opinions were held the expected demise of the Wilmot
Proviso could not arouse any enthusiasm for expansion.

It appears, then, that the slavery question which during
the first year of the war acted in most instances as a deterrent to the forces of expansion, was by the fall of 1847 no
longer such an obstacle to the acquisition of territory. Increasing numbers of people at the North were becoming convinced that the Wilmot Proviso was not an indispensable
prerequisite for the addition of free territory to the Union.
Such being the state of public opinion, would-be presidential
candidates among northern Democrats, who had been forced
to exercise caution at the beginning of the war, could now
condemn the Wilmot Proviso and enlarge their schemes of
conquest without fear of committing political suicide. On
the other hand, at the South there were evidences that
opposition to the acquisition of territory was increasing. In
so far as slavery was a determining factor, northern approval
and southern disapproval of expansion were based on a common belief that slave institutions could not be extended into
the territory which the expansionists were proposing to annex.
This belief had been gradually established by propaganda
during 1847. It cannot be maintained that generalizations
on this subject are any more valid than generalizations on
any other subject. In the Southwest for instance, the Wilmot Proviso seems never to have caused any great amount of
alarm.[139] Moreover, many southerners were perfectly satisfied, provided the Wilmot Proviso were not adopted, to
acquire all the territory it was possible to secure. On the
whole it may be said that in the fall of 1847 conditions
were more favorable for expansion than at any time since the
beginning of the war. Just at this juncture events in Mexico
seemed to play into the hands of the expansionists with the
result that the movement for the absorption of all Mexico
became a recognizable force in the United States.

---

[139] See for instance the New Orleans *Picayune*, 14 January 1848.
On December 26, 1847, J. D. B. DeBow wrote Calhoun from New
Orleans: "The strength of feeling in opposition to the Proviso here
though not as great as in South Carolina is marked." *Correspondence Addressed to Calhoun*, p. 415.

CHAPTER III

GROWTH

The appearance of a widespread sentiment for the absorption of all Mexico was due to the cumulative effect of several events and conditions. The mere length of the war and the development of war psychology tended to make the American people more bombastic in expression and more impatient in feeling toward Mexico. The war, which it was generally believed would be of short duration, seemed no nearer to an end in September, 1847, than at the beginning of hostilities. The notable victories of the American armies in 1847 and the persistent refusal of Mexico to agree to satisfactory terms of peace further inflamed the minds of super-patriots and apostles of manifest destiny. As has already been noted, through the spring and summer of 1847 there appeared numerous expressions of belief that the war was tending toward the destruction of the independence of Mexico. In many cases, no doubt, such belief was merely the public manifestation of an ardent desire to acquire Mexico. Moreover, many at the North were becoming convinced that it was not necessary to insist on the principles of the Wilmot Proviso in order to exclude slavery from any territory acquired from Mexico. This made it somewhat easier for large ideas of expansion to develop. It must be said, however, that extremists in both the anti-slavery and pro-slavery camps were never satisfied and continued to inject the slavery issue into all discussions concerning territorial indemnity from Mexico.

In the fall of 1847 further developments both in the course of the war and in domestic politics gave rise to a clear expression of the desire for all Mexico. The breakdown in the negotiations between Trist and the Mexicans, the capture of Mexico City by General Scott on September 14, and the Democratic gains in the fall elections in the United States, produced a definite sentiment for the absorption of Mexico. The apparent failure of Trist demonstrated to the satisfaction of the expansionists that peace on "honorable" terms was impossible of realization. At the same time the capture of the capital of Mexico laid the whole country at the feet of the Anglo-Saxon conquerors. Why should the United States not go on and fulfill its "mission"? The gods seemed to have intervened in favor of the imperialists, who might now not only civilize the benighted Mexicans but also, incidentally of course, secure vast commercial and industrial advantages. This happy state of affairs could be charged to the foolish obstinacy of the Mexicans rather than to imperialistic designs of the United States. In addition, Democratic successes especially in Maine, Rhode Island, Vermont and Pennsylvania were interpreted to mean that the people were ready to support a more drastic program against Mexico.[1] Politicians could now formulate extensive plans of conquest without too much danger. These various influences worked together to produce a sentiment which boded ill for Mexico.

Beginning in October the tone of the press indicated that the organs of the expansionists were convinced that the Mexican embroglio would end in the absorption of Mexico by the United States. Expressions of alarm from sources opposed to extensive acquisitions of territory furnish additional evidence that the expansionists were thought to be correct in their estimate of the probabilities of the case. Some members of the administration began to advocate the complete subjugation and permanent occupation of the whole or a greater part of Mexico. Officers in the army recommended the same procedure. It was noised abroad that a large party in Mexico desired a permanent connection with the United States. In the Congress which assembled in December, 1847, the question of the fate of Mexico received considerable attention for the first time. During the first part of the session the discussions generally consisted of expressions of alarm from those who were opposed to extensive annexations, and

---

[1] Boston *Post*, 18 September 1847; Charleston *Mercury*, quoted by *Niles, Register*, LXXIII, 160; Buchanan to Trist, 7, 24 October 1847, Trist MSS. For the results of the Pennsylvania election which seemed to have much influence on Buchanan and Dallas, see *Niles' Register*, LXXIII, 112, 128.

very emphatic denials of any desire to acquire Mexico from those who doubtless were not so reluctant as they appeared to be. A presidential campaign was in the offing and public opinion had not yet become sufficiently clear to warrant the taking of a definite and unequivocal stand by aspiring politicians.

With the approach of the new year there can be noticed a further development of expansionist sentiment. From January until the appearance of the Treaty of Guadalupe Hidalgo at Washington in the latter part of February, the sentiment for the absorption of Mexico may be said to have reached its period of greatest development. The action of forces emanating from the administration, Congress and the press, stimulating each other, was gradually creating a strong sentiment in favor of the acquisition of Mexico. The attitude of the politicians became less ambiguous and their denials less emphatic along with this crystallization of public opinion. Gatherings which assumed the character of revival meetings created enthusiasm for the idea of " rescuing " the Mexicans. There were indications that some of the abolitionists would not look with disfavor on the absorption of all Mexico. In short all the omens pointed toward the demise of the Mexican republic when the treaty of peace was received at Washington on February 19. It shortly appeared that Mexico was to be given another chance to exist as an independent nation.

Press comments in New England in the fall of 1847 reflected, or perhaps foreshadowed, these new developments of public opinion. To the Boston *Post,* Whig losses in New England indicated that there was a " sound Americanism at the north that has not been appealed to in vain." The *Post* did not at the time commit itself on the question of the absorption of Mexico, but the great glee with which the editor commented on the downfall of the " no territory " platform of the Whigs was indicative of the current trend of opinion.[2] In a short time the Boston daily would be proclaiming the " mighty mission of the unthralled Saxon." [3] Fully as sig-

---

[2] Boston *Post*, 18 September 1847.   [3] *Ibid.*, 1 February 1848.

nificant was the attitude of the *New Englander*. This journal had for commercial, humanitarian and religious reasons
approved the acquisition of California and New Mexico.[4] In
October, 1847, however, the editor thought that the war might
bring larger additions of territory. After so much slaughter
on both sides, peace seemed as far away as ever. " The omens
indicate that we are entering upon the career of conquest
. . . and that our people are to be infected more and more
with the vulgar robber passion of military adventure." In
other words, faced with the possibility, perhaps the probability, of the absorption of Mexico, the *New Englander* gave
expression to the old distaste of the Northeast for westward
extension on account of its adverse effect on the relative
power of the eastern seaboard. The only hope lay in an early
return of the dove of peace, but the bird seemed to have been
delayed on his return flight. " God of our Fathers ! " wailed
the editor, " give us peace ! Oh what results for us and the
world, are involved in the return of that inestimable blessing." [5] But there was no peace, and the likelihood of the
acquisition of Mexico became more and more evident.

In New York leading papers were busily engaged in creating a public sentiment in favor of the absorption of Mexico.
The agricultural and mineral resources of that country, and
the value of a canal or a railroad across the Isthmus of
Tehuantepac were described in glowing terms.[6] Mexico, who
could not make war and would not make peace, must accept
the responsibility for her own downfall.

It is a gorgeous prospect, this annexation of all Mexico. It were
more desirable that she should come to us voluntarily; but as we
shall have no peace until she be annexed, let it come, even though
force be necessary, at first to bring her. Like the Sabine virgins,
she will soon learn to love her ravishers.[7]

Anyhow it was useless to oppose the dictates of Providence,
who had " willed this war to unite and exalt both nations."

---

[4] *New Englander*, V, 141-142.
[5] *Ibid.*, pp. 604-605, 613.
[6] New York *Herald*, 19 October 1847; New York *Sun*, quoted by
Niles' Register, LXXIII, 113; *Democratic Review*, XXI, 388-389.
[7] New York *Herald*, 8 October 1847.

This result was "as certain and inevitable as any event in human history."[8] More ambiguous was the attitude of the *Democratic Review* whose editor recommended the "occupation" of Mexico. It was admitted that occupation would be followed by the entrance of Anglo-Saxon settlers which would result in bringing Mexico "piece by piece" into the Union. Yet this did not mean the "direct and permanent annexation of the country to the United States."[9] These statements could be interpreted as the reader desired, but however interpreted the actual result of a long continued occupation would have been the end of the Mexican republic. It was a propaganda appealing to necessity, idealism and greed which the press issued to the people. Of course the war was not being waged to get control of the wealth of Mexico. The obstinacy of the Mexicans and the machinations of the celestial powers were responsible for the situation which made it necessary that the United States assume control of the southern republic with all its material advantages. In such manner was furnished an appeal broad enough to influence very diverse elements of public opinion.

Pennsylvanians and Marylanders read stories with substantially the same theme. The Philadelphia *Ledger's* Washington correspondent informed the public that there was no longer any government in Mexico and that a group of Mexicans was anxious to have the United States "keep military possession of the country, as the only means of protecting their lives and property."

We must be prepared for a bold move, such as will place the military chieftains of Mexico entirely *hors du combat*, and that, disguise it as we may, *will be the final subjugation and annexation, after a certain period, of all Mexico.* The administration is gradually coming to it, though not without hesitation; but the force of circumstances is greater than all predeterminations on the part of the administration.[10]

---

[8] New York *Sun*, quoted by Dodd, *The West and the War with Mexico*, pp. 163-164.
[9] *Democratic Review*, XXI, 291, 381, 389.
[10] Philadelphia *Ledger*, quoted by the Boston *Post*, 29 November 1847.

The Whig Baltimore *American* also declared that "in high official quarters" the occupation and annexation of Mexico was being discussed. Secretary Walker was "known to favor wholesale occupancy and annexation." The *American* viewed with alarm a war of indefinite duration which it thought might end with the annexation of all the Mexican territory.[11] The man in the street, whose opinions were influenced and indeed formed largely by the newspapers, was being told that there was no government in Mexico; that some of the Mexicans desired the United States to take control of their country; that the Washington government was considering such a step; that the sum total of events pointed to the extinction of the independence of Mexico. Sooner or later such ideas would become a part of popular psychology, and if conditions remained the same the absorption of Mexico would be a foregone conclusion.

Of particular interest and significance was the attitude of the *National Whig.* Early in November this paper which was ardently supporting the political interests of General Taylor, outlined the policy which should be followed by the United States. Since it was evident that Mexico was determined not to listen to reason, the Washington government should declare at once:

> It is, therefore, declared, for the peace and quiet of this land, [Mexico] for the happiness of these people, and to end the effusion of human blood, *that the United States, from this day forward, ends the war—assumes the entire conquest of Mexico—annexes it to the United States,* and the people are required to repair to their respective homes, and there await the call of the proper authorities of their different States to organize their several State Constitutions, which, if Republican, will be accepted into the Union. . . . All in default, acting contrary to this manifesto, be traitors, whose lives and property will be confiscated.[12]

It would be difficult to imagine a program more definite and thoroughgoing. No paper had heretofore been so explicit, and curiously enough this came from the supporter of a Whig

---

[11] Baltimore *American*, quoted by *Niles' Register*, LXXIII, 113.
[12] *National Whig*, 10 November 1847.

candidate for the presidential nomination,[13] in the evident belief that a candidate could win on such a platform. It seems fairly certain that the people were not prepared for the absorption of Mexico in November, 1847. But it is almost equally certain that they would have been by the time of the next presidential election had the war not ended in the meantime. The *National Whig* was widely quoted, especially in the West.[14] This sheet, which according to the Detroit *Free Press* "may be regarded as the organ of a large proportion, if not a decided majority of one of the great parties of the country," [15] had stolen the thunder of the Democratic expansionists with a vengeance. While the *Free Press* exaggerated the influence of the *National Whig,* still it is clear that the number of converts to the idea of the annexation of Mexico was steadily growing.

The increasing probability of the absorption of Mexico was causing more and more disquietude to the southeastern slavocracy. Wilson Lumpkin, a prominent Georgia Democrat, was very dubious about what was to follow in the wake of the Mexican War. He did not think that a territory thickly populated with Mexicans ought to be annexed. The "whole letter and spirit of our Government stands opposed to conquering provinces to govern, or to . . . conquering a country for the purpose of annexation to our Union." [16] To Governor Johnson, of South Carolina, the annexation of Mexico meant that "a contest more disastrous than the war itself" would take place on the subject of slavery. Furthermore, the gover-

---

[13] Taylor, himself, did not advocate the annexation of Mexico. At one time he was apparently willing to take all the territory east of the Sierra Madre Mountains, but later he became more moderate. This change was caused by the slavery issue and the exigencies of his position as a Whig candidate for the presidential nomination. Taylor to Crittenden, 9 October 1846, 3 January 1848, Crittenden MSS; Sheafe to Webster, 20 January 1848, Webster MSS; *Niles' Register,* LXXIII, 400.

[14] New Orleans *Picayune,* 26 May 1847; Washington Correspondent of the New York *Herald,* 19 October 1847; Detroit *Free Press,* 10 November 1847.

[15] Detroit *Free Press,* 10 November 1847.

[16] Lumpkin to Calhoun, 18 November 1847, *Correspondence of Calhoun,* p. 1135.

nor did not believe that Mexico was worth what it would cost in dollars and cents to conquer her.[17] The Nashville *Union* undertook to assure its readers that " no considerable body of men in the country advocate the annexation of any portion of Mexico, except Upper California and New Mexico." [18] This is direct evidence that there was opposition to the annexation of Mexico at the South, as well as a tacit admission that a demand for extensive annexations did exist somewhere. Waddy Thompson was greatly alarmed to see " that the madness which rules the hour is increasing and seems literally to grow by what it feeds on." The Carolinian did not believe that England and France would " consent to our subjugating Mexico." Even if they did, to annex that country " would ipso facto dissolve the Union." [19] The Charleston *Mercury* joined the chorus by calling on the people of the United States to beware of eating the " forbidden fruit," which in this case was the Mexican apple. To do so *" would be to subject our institutions to political death."* [20] As will be seen later it was Calhoun who took the lead in opposing the absorption of Mexico in the Thirtieth Congress. Some of those slaveholders, who, if certain northern Whigs and abolitionists were to be believed, were engaged in a war to extend slavery, did not seem enthusiastic over the prospect before them.

While dissatisfaction was undoubtedly the dominant note with which the eastern slaveholders greeted the possibility of the absorption of all Mexico, there was, nevertheless, some dissenting opinion. All did not agree that slavery could not be introduced into Mexican territory. In fact it was declared in some quarters that extensive annexation was the only salvation for the institution. The Mobile *Herald* thought that after slavery was abolished in the border states great numbers of slaves would be concentrated in the far South, where their very numbers would make them insubordinate and profitless.

---

[17] Charleston *Mercury*, 23 November 1847.
[18] Nashville *Union*, 10 December 1847.
[19] Thompson to Calhoun, 18 December 1847, *Correspondence of Calhoun*, pp. 1149-1150.
[20] Charleston *Mercury*, 30 December 1847.

These evils may be avoided by taking new territory adapted to slave labor; or indeed by taking any kind of territory in the direction of Mexico. The profitable existence of slavery is by no means incompatible with a more temperate region but it is incompatible with a very dense population. We need plenty of soil to render it valuable.[21]

In his annual message to the Virginia legislature Governor Smith declared that territory acquired from Mexico would be a natural outlet for slaves from Virginia and other southern states. As the population of a state became more dense slave labor would become less profitable. Consequently room should be secured in which slavery could "diffuse itself." "The South never can consent to be confined to prescribed limits. She wants and must have space, if consistent with honor and propriety."[22] Where views like these were held there was not likely to be any great opposition to the annexation of all Mexico. However, there seems to have been less support for the idea of extensive annexations of Mexican territory in the Southeast than in any other section of the Union, except perhaps New England.

But the people of the Southwest exhibited little anxiety on the subject of slavery in Mexican territory. They were expansionists first and slaveholders afterward. In fact the whole West—North and South, slave states as well as free states—seemed ready to approve the policy of a complete dismemberment of Mexico.[23] When the news that Mexico had refused to agree to American proposals for peace became public, a large meeting of citizens was held at New Orleans for the purpose of assuring the government support in a vigorous prosecution of the war. It was declared that any "American who would require his Government to offer peace again would be proclaimed a traitor."[24] The public mind was apparently becoming convinced of the necessity of a permanent occupation of Mexico.[25] The New Orleans *Bee* and the *Picayune*

---

[21] Mobile *Herald*, quoted by the Charleston *Mercury*, 28 September 1847.

[22] *Niles' Register*, LXXIII, 290-291.

[23] Dodd, pp. 162-163.

[24] New Orleans *Picayune*, 30 September, 1 October 1847.

[25] Anonymous letter in *De Bow's Review*, IV, 95.

toyed with the idea of the absorption of Mexico. According to the *Bee,* " the arrogance and imbecility of Mexico . . . bids fair to abridge the process by which her absorption and ultimate denationalization will be accomplished." Since Mexico was doomed to come under the sway of the United States, it might be well in the meantime to prepare the Mexicans " for the appreciation of the fate in store for them." [26] The *Picayune* contended that the United States was not bound by the objects avowed at the beginning of hostilities as certain rights of conquest and occupation had been acquired since. No one could " say now that the only way of making a peace is not to conquer and rule over the whole country." In her great weakness Mexico was likely to " fall into the arms of a European dynasty." Moreover, the better order of the Mexicans did not want the United States to withdraw from their country.[27]

The story as here told has a familiar ring. Much the same sort of material was appearing in eastern newspapers. Necessity, fear of Europe, inevitability and the approval of the better classes in Mexico were invoked to prepare the inhabitants of the Southwest for the absorption of Mexico. And they needed little preparation. There seemed to be not quite so much emphasis on the economic advantages of Mexico as in the East, although there was much interest in the commercial future of New Orleans. It was thought that a railroad across Mexico and extensive territorial acquisitions would assure the future greatness of the Louisiana metropolis—all the more reason why Mexico should be dismembered.[28] The hardy expansionists of the Southwest were not deterred by fear of " danger to American institutions " or by misgivings about the slavery issue. All such questions would settle themselves in time.

Farther to the north a like propaganda was being offered to the public. The war correspondent of the St. Louis *Repub-*

---

[26] New Orleans *Bee,* quoted by the *National Whig,* 2 November 1847.

[27] New Orleans *Picayune,* 27, 28 November, 8 December 1847.

[28] *De Bow's Review,* III, 107-108, 475-478, 485-486, 495.

lican wrote from Mexico that among wealthy and respectable Mexicans there was a strong desire that the United States take over Mexico rather than leave the job for some European country. The result, said the writer, " is the best that possibly can follow, both to Mexico and the United States." [29] The Illinois *State Register* and the Detroit *Free Press* continued to urge conquest, subjugation, and the annihilation of Mexican sovereignty as the only alternative if Mexico refused to make a peace based on a fair indemnity. Every American citizen would insist upon it to the last ditch.[30] The West with its intense nationalism, its ardent belief in the glorious destiny of the United States, and its impatience with the protracted peace negotiations seemed ready to remove Mexico from the list of independent nations.[31]

The contemporaneous maneuvers of the leaders in the Whig party indicated that the absorption of Mexico was becoming a question which required the attention of politicians. On November 13, Henry Clay delivered an oration and proposed a set of resolutions at Lexington, Kentucky. Clay's theme was opposition to the war and to the policy of the administration. He declared that Polk had been responsible for the beginning of hostilities, and suggested that Congress determine what should be the objects of the war. If the President refused to conform to the wishes of Congress, steps should be taken to bring hostilities to a close. While Clay did not attribute to Polk the design " of conquering and annexing Mexico, in all its boundless extent," yet he confessed himself " shocked and alarmed by manifestations of it in various quarters." This movement Clay condemned in no uncertain terms and intimated that a proper boundary for Texas was all that should be required from Mexico.[32] Albert Gallatin soon followed suit, taking much the same stand as Clay. Gal-

---

[29] St. Louis *Republican*, quoted by the Illinois *State Register*, 26 November 1847.

[30] *Illinois State Register*, 5 November 1847; Detroit *Free Press*, 10 November 1847.

[31] Dodd, pp. 162-163.

[32] Clay's speech and resolutions may be found in *Niles' Register*, LXXIII, 190, 197-200.

latin did not believe "that the executive will favor the wild suggestions of a subjugation of the whole of Mexico, or any of its interior provinces. . . ."[33] Be that as it may, there were many people who did favor "wild suggestions" or a politician like Henry Clay would never have broached a subject so full of dynamite. His apparent effort to relieve Polk of any designs on all Mexico was probably no more than an attempt to create the opposite impression.

There is little doubt but that Clay was attempting to provide a platform for the Whigs in the next presidential campaign with himself as standard-bearer, and many Whigs responded nobly to his efforts.[34] Others, however, seemed to think that the party's chances of success on such a platform were very slight. The *National Whig,* having already proposed the absorption of Mexico, expressed the belief that "if the Whig party make Mr. Clay's policy national Whig policy, and go before the country upon it, they will be signally defeated by the public voice."[35] A New York Whig wrote Judge McLean:

> The people of the U. S. will not sustain, *any man*, entertaining such opinions, as put forth in those [Clay's] resolutions. . . . Democracy, alias, the democratic side, of the Mexican War question, is the popular Side, hence it will be the *right side* and the one also that will elect the next Presit provided always, if the war is continued and the limits of Slavery, are fixed. I am for holding on to all the power and advantages that we have obtained in Mexico. . . .[36]

A little later the same writer declared:

> The people ask, shall we take a man, for the Presity who, is opposed, to this Mexican War, or shall we, select one, who is for holding on, to the whole advantages, we now possess; and if this enemy, will not render us, ample justice, compel it, to do so, by force of arms. . . . The people, it appears, have already decided, in their cool, quiet, unpretending way, to go for the man, that will carry on, this Mexican War.[37]

---

[33] *Ibid.*, p. 239.
[34] Calvin Colton, *The Last Seven Years of the Life of Henry Clay,* pp. 72-73.
[35] *National Whig,* 17 November 1847.
[36] J. B. Mower to McLean, 22 November 1847, McLean MSS. It will be noted that the writer apparently assumes that there will be little difficulty in fixing the limits of slavery. This represents a view which was rapidly gaining strength at the North.
[37] 13 December 1847, *ibid.*

Another friend of McLean's reported that there were thousands of good Whigs who did not approve of Clay's sentiments in regard to the war. The writer thought that the Kentuckian's resolutions were insincere and did "not deserve the approval of Whigs who love their own country better than Mexico." [38]

Nothing better illustrates the gradual development of public opinion than these comments on Clay's platform. The commentators were politicians and they were interested in supplying Judge McLean with a statement of principles which would prove successful in the coming presidential campaign.[39] In their opinion the "no territory" and "no supply" cries of the Whigs had put the party out of harmony with the general trend of events. This did not mean that the Whig party, or any considerable proportion of it, was ready to propose the absorption of Mexico. But it did mean that some of the Whigs were beginning to believe that the expansionists were riding on the crest of the wave of public opinion. Already such Whig organs as the New Orleans *Bee* and the *National Whig* had suggested the annexation of Mexico. What else could be expected of the Democrats?

Meanwhile, what had been happening in administration circles? It will be recalled that early in September Polk had

---

[38] Thomas Dowling to McLean, 7 December 1847, *ibid.*

[39] Judge McLean refused to take the stand suggested by some of his friends. On January 7, 1848, he issued a statement almost identical in principle with Clay's platform. Cincinnati *Gazette*, quoted by the Charleston *Mercury*, 1 February 1848. As a result McLean received a rather interesting letter from a Michigan Whig: "I am a farmer & Illiterate though I have perused your letter on the Mexican war with mortification & regret [.] you have stated over your own signiture that the war was unnessecarly & unconstitutionally commenced by the Presideut [.] now is this statement true [?] far from it [.] In your zeal to bring yourself before the public as a candidate for the Presidency you stated what every man of common sence knows to be false when you penned the letter [.] Do you imagine Sir that the whig party is so destitute of love of country & patriotism that they will run after tratars to thier owen country. . . . Mr Clay killed himself by writing obnoxious letter and you are following suit." J. W. Wood to McLean, 3 March 1848, McLean MSS. This letter has all the earmarks of being a hoax. Some of the words and expressions are rather inconsistent with a state of illiteracy. But the sentiment expressed was beginning to permeate Whig ranks.

apparently decided to demand more territory if the news from Mexico continued to be unfavorable. And the news was destined to be decidedly unsatisfactory. On August 27, the first meeting between Trist and the Mexicans took place.[40] It soon developed that there was little possibility of an agreement on the basis of the American demands. Mexico demanded that the territory between the Nueces and the Rio Grande be neutralized with neither country allowed to make a settlement in it. She also refused to grant a right of transit across the Isthmus of Tehuantepec or to cede Lower California, New Mexico and a part of Upper California. The American commissioner agreed to refer the question of the Nueces-Rio Grande country to Washington if the Mexicans would consent to surrender Upper California and New Mexico for a money payment. Nothing came of this, however, and on September 6, negotiations were abandoned.[41] News of these happenings was not likely to reassure Polk. Especially would the President be offended by Trist's offer to refer the matter of the Nueces boundary to Washington. Many of the Whigs had been constantly asserting that the territory between the Nueces and the Rio Grande belonged to Mexico. Trist's action tended to lend some color to the Whig contention. If that territory did not belong to the United States, then the thesis of Mexico's war guilt had no foundation in fact and the President of the United States was convicted of making false statements.

Before receiving official information of the result of the negotiations in Mexico, Polk had determined to recall Trist. On October 2, unofficial news was received at Washington which convinced the President that Mexico " has refused to treat for peace upon terms which the U. S. can accept." [42] Trist was recalled, so Polk said, because

his remaining longer with the army could not, probably, accomplish the objects of his mission, and because his remaining longer might,

---

[40] Trist to Buchanan, 29 August 1847, Trist MSS.
[41] For the early negotiations, see McCormac, *James K. Polk*, pp. 515-517; Smith, *The War with Mexico*, II, 135-138.
[42] Polk's *Diary*, III, 186; Buchanan to Trist, 6 October 1847, Trist MSS.

& probably would, impress the Mexican Government with the belief that the U. S. were so anxious for peace that they would ultimate[ly] conclude one upon the Mexican terms.[43]

The initiative in making efforts for peace was to be transferred to the Mexican government, and at the same time General Scott was ordered to levy contributions on the enemy for the support of the American army.[44]

It seems probable that had Polk's policy as regards further negotiations been carried out Mexico would now be a part of the United States. It was hard enough to get the Mexicans to negotiate even with continual urging by a representative on the ground. There is little likelihood that any Mexican government would have taken the initiative in proposing satisfactory terms of peace until it was too late to preserve their independence. If manifestations of public opinion in the United States meant anything, Mexico would not have a great deal of time in which to make up her mind. And a party in Mexico had already made up its mind that the United States should take charge of the country.[45] Yet it is hard to blame Polk for his action in the case and there is no reason to believe that his motives as given in the diary were not sincere.[46] Although he was probably wrong, the President had reached the conclusion that if his negotiator remained in Mexico the achievement of peace would be rendered more difficult. As it turned out, Trist did not obey his instructions concerning the discontinuance of negotiations. His refusal to do so seems to have been an essential factor in preventing the absorption of Mexico.

---

[43] Polk's *Diary*, III, 186. It is probable that Polk had a slight suspicion that the reports concerning his commissioner's action in regard to the Nueces boundary were true. This would make him all the more anxious to recall Trist. Buchanan, however, stated in his letter of recall that reports on that subject were not believed in Washington. Yet this unofficial information on other matters was considered as sufficient evidence to warrant the recall of Trist. Buchanan to Trist, 6 October 1847, Trist MSS.

[44] Buchanan to Trist, 6 October 1847, Trist MSS; Marcy to Scott, 6 October 1847, *30th Cong., 1st sess., S. Doc. No. 52*, pp. 138-139; McCormac, pp. 518-519.

[45] Smith, II, 125, 234, 323.

[46] McCormac, p. 519.

Since it was naturally not expected at Washington that Trist in spite of his recall would continue his efforts for a treaty, it was necessary that the administration formulate a policy to be presented to Congress in December. While the question was being mooted by the President and his cabinet, various forces tending toward the absorption of Mexico were brought to bear on the administration. Manifestations in the press and the Whig defeats in the elections of 1847 convinced such politicians as Secretary Buchanan that the American people were in no mood to trifle with Mexico.[47] It behooved candidates for the presidential nomination to take note of the state of public opinion. Then, too, army officers presented suggestions which directly or indirectly pointed toward the annexation of Mexico. Said General Persifer Smith:

> We have done all the opinion of the world demanded of us here, [in Mexico] and are now at liberty to consult solely our *own interest*, subject of course to the law of Nations. Let [us] therefore pay ourselves at once, by taking from our enemy what it is our interest to have and our right to take. . . .[48]

Much more explicit was General Worth:

> That our race is finally destined to overrun the whole continent is too obvious to need proof. . . . After much reflection I have arrived at the conclusion that it is our decided policy to hold the whole of Mexico,—The details of occupation are comparatively unimportant— I mean by occupation, *permanent conquest* and future annexation. . . .[49]

In December General Quitman also advised permanent military occupation of Mexico. This, he said, could be done without expense to the United States and without serious opposition from the people of Mexico.[50] Moreover, George Bancroft,

---

[47] In October Buchanan wrote Trist: " . . . after all the blood and treasure which have been expended since the date of your instructions, a Treaty founded on the ultimatum of your instructions, especially if the maximum is to be paid, would not be popular. The spirit of this country is now thoroughly aroused." Buchanan to Trist, 24 October 1847, Trist MSS.

[48] Trist in a letter to Buchanan enclosed this communication from Smith. Buchanan evidently turned over the letter to Secretary of War, Marcy. The letter dated September 28, 1847, may be found in the Marcy MSS.

[49] Worth to Marcy, 30 October 1847, Marcy MSS.

[50] J. F. H. Claiborne, ed., *Life and Correspondence of General John A. Quitman*, II, 7; J. Fred Rippy, *The United States and Mexico*, p. 16.

who had already decided that it would be best to take a
"very huge slice" of Mexico,[51] wrote Polk from England
that it was becoming a fashion there to expect the absorption
of Mexico. "Though you annex all Mexico," continued the
minister, "England will not trouble herself much about
it. . . ."[52] Doubtless the Washington officials also took cog-
nizance of the existence of an annexationist movement in
Mexico.[53]

At best these forces did not tend to moderate the policy of
the administration. Here was public opinion "thoroughly
aroused"; army officers, as much politicians as soldiers,
recommending the absorption of Mexico; the American minister at London, himself convinced that the next presidential
campaign would turn on that issue, reporting that England
expected and would not oppose the annexation of Mexico by
the United States; and reports from south of the Rio Grande
that annexation had supporters among the Mexican people.
It was to be expected that the expansionist Walker and that
barometer of public opinion, James Buchanan, would in-
stantly react to such unmistakable signs. And so they did.
The President and the other members of the cabinet were
affected also, but not as much as Walker and Buchanan.

Cabinet discussions in connection with the preparation of
the President's annual message to Congress revealed the effect
of the progress of events. On November 9, Buchanan's tone
was "unsettled." He said that Polk in his message must
either designate what part of Mexico would be taken as indemnity, or suggest the occupation and subjugation of the
whole country. The Secretary would not commit himself as
to which of these two courses was preferable but Polk gathered
that "he would favour the policy of acquiring in addition to

---

[51] "So Santa Anna will not or cannot make peace. '*The whole of
Mexico*' (meaning a very huge slice) becomes the Watchword; and
the next Presidential contest will turn on that question inevitably."
Bancroft to Donelson, 26 October 1847, Donelson MSS.

[52] Bancroft to Polk, 18 November 1847, *Life and Letters of Bancroft*, II, 28.

[53] Trist to Buchanan, 25 October 1847, Trist MSS; Parrott [from
Vera Cruz] to Marcy, 20 December 1847, Marcy MSS.

California and New Mexico, the Province of Tamaulipas and
the country East of the Sierra Madre mountains." [54] This
was a rather sudden change for a man who had been insisting
that no more than California and New Mexico should be
acquired and who at the outset of the war had wanted to
inform Europe that no territory would be taken. But such
are the exigencies of politics that much must be forgiven a
would-be presidential candidate. As for Polk, he declared
that the Californias and New Mexico would never be restored
to Mexico, and that if war continued further indemnity must
be demanded.[55] Buchanan had passed the President in the
race for Mexican territory, but Polk left the way open for
further advances if Mexico continued to be recalcitrant.

During the next two weeks work continued on the annual
message. In Buchanan's draft of a paragraph on the Mexican
policy the Secretary declared that if all measures failed to
obtain peace " we must fulfill that destiny which Providence
may have in store for both countries." [56] Polk thought this
statement too vague, but all the members of the cabinet except the Attorney-General seemed to agree that " Providence "
was the safest guide to follow.[57] Walker favored Buchanan's
wording because he concluded, naturally enough, that a majority of the people would think that it meant the absorption
of Mexico, which was entirely in accord with his personal
views.[58] Polk was opposed to going to any such lengths. Furthermore, he did not desire that his message " should be so
obscure as to give rise to doubt or discussions. . . ." [59] Unfortunately for the President, whatever may have been his
intentions, the message as finally prepared did give rise to
almost endless discussions as to his real intentions. Although
Buchanan's language was altered, the changes made were

---

[54] Polk's *Diary*, III, 216-218; Bourne, *American Historical Review*,
V, 494; McCormac, pp. 527-528.
[55] *Ibid.*   [56] Polk's *Diary*, III, 226.   [57] Bourne, p. 495.
[58] Polk's *Diary*, III, 229. Walker attempted to reveal his views to
Congress, but Polk insisted that the treasury report should not vio-
late the spirit of his own message. Bourne, p. 495.
[59] Polk's *Diary*, III, 229.

vague enough. Except for the fact that the aid of Providence was not invoked to provide for all eventualities in the final draft, there was not much difference in substance between the two statements.

Put in plain terms the situation was something like this: Walker definitely wanted to take all Mexico and made no secret of the fact; Buchanan just as definitely intended to shape his course according to the state of public opinion, which apparently was pointing in that direction; the other members of the cabinet with the exception of Attorney-General Clifford were also willing to be guided by the voice of the people, which was more euphemistically designated as the dictates of Providence; Polk did not intend to rely on divine revelation as expounded by the public, but he did intend to get indemnity from Mexico and the size of this indemnity would be measured by the length of the war. It seems that the failure of Trist and the drift of public opinion were causing members of the administration to demand increased cessions of territory, although this apparently affected the President less than any of his advisers. On the other hand, rumors that the administration was considering the annexation of Mexico were spread abroad and tended to point public opinion more directly toward that goal. Truly, Mexico's position seemed to be steadily growing more precarious since she had declined Trist's propositions on September 6.

The message which had been causing so much commotion in the cabinet was presented to Congress on December 7. The President reminded the legislators that the Californias and New Mexico had been in the possession of the United States since the early months of the war. He was " satisfied that they should never be surrendered to Mexico." But there were in addition other provinces which had been conquered by American troops. The fate of these territories " must depend on the future progress of the war, and the course which Mexico may think proper hereafter to pursue." For the benefit of doubters Polk declared: " It has never been contemplated by me, as an object of the war, to make a permanent conquest of the Republic of Mexico, or to annihilate her separate existence as an independent nation. . . ." Then what was to be done? The Chief Executive asserted that the American forces might be compelled to set up and maintain a republican government in Mexico " willing to conclude a peace which would be just to them and secure us the indemnity we demand." If this should fail to produce the desired results, " then we shall have exhausted all honorable means in pursuit of peace, and must continue to occupy her country with our troops, taking the full measure of indemnity into our own hands, and must enforce the terms which our honor demands." It is hard to distinguish any real difference between this last passage and the statement of Buchanan which it replaced. Both were indefinite and could be interpreted by a reasonable man to mean that if peace were not secured soon all Mexico would be taken. Finally the President recommended a vigorous prosecution of the war and called for additional troops to serve in Mexico.[60]

A comparison of this message with the one delivered a year earlier will give a fairly good indication of what had been taking place in the meantime. In 1846, Polk had declared that the war was not being waged " with a view to conquest." [61] But in December, 1847, the President felt it necessary to state that he had no intention of conquering all Mexico. In his second annual message Polk had only by

---

[60] Cong. Globe, 30th Cong., 1st sess., pp. 6-8. After reading Polk's message, the Whig Professor Lieber of South Carolina College, wrote what he called " An Ode to the American People and Congress." Dr. Lieber's theme was the glorious destiny of the United States and the necessity of a ship canal to " make the ocean free." De Bow's Review, V, 388-390. Apparently the professor thought that the President's sentiments as expressed in the message were not incompatible with the theme of the poem. One Democratic expansionist organ undertook to congratulate Dr. Lieber. " This is a good sign, as the Dr. distinctly realizes the mighty mission of the unthralled Saxon. Wherever a whig has soul and sense enough to elevate him above the slough of his party, his mind attains at once the natural scope and grandeur of democracy." Boston Post, 1 February 1848. The editor probably meant the " grandeur " of the Democratic party. These effusions were among the indirect results of the message which Polk intended should not be so obscure as to lead to doubt and discussions.

[61] For the message of 1846, see above, p. 53.

implication suggested the permanent retention of California and New Mexico, whereas the third message distinctly stated that those territories ought never be returned to Mexico and intimated that if the war continued other provinces in the hands of the United States troops should be taken as indemnity. The President suggested in 1846 that the war be prosecuted vigorously to obtain an " honorable peace " and " ample indemnity," while in 1847 the possibility of the necessity of establishing a government in Mexico under American auspices was recognized. If this failed to secure peace, the continued occupation of the country and a " full measure of indemnity " would be in order. The lapse of time did not seem to be in Mexico's favor.

Thus the President, while disclaiming any intention of acquiring Mexico, left the way open for ever-increasing amounts of territorial indemnity. In fact, as a last resort, he recommended measures which, though perhaps not intended for that purpose, must inevitably have led to the absorption of the southern republic. The setting up of a government by the American forces and the continued occupation of the country were measures recommended by many who thought that the annexation of Mexico was inevitable. They realized that such measures would achieve that end. That Polk did not reach the same conclusion is hard to believe. One suspects that the President was ready to take Mexico if his peace measures failed, though there is no evidence to show that he was anxious to do so, or that his policy was shaped with that end in view.

The Congress which assembled in December, 1847, was composed of a Whig House and a Democratic Senate. It has generally been supposed that the fact that the House of Representatives was controlled by the opposition was an important factor in preserving the independence of Mexico.[62] This contention may well be doubted. Many of the Whigs were interested in securing territorial indemnity from Mexico and their number was increasing. Public opinion was such

---

[62] Bourne, p. 502; Dodd, p. 165.

that the House did not dare to refuse the necessary supplies
for the army, although it was feared by the administration
that this might happen.[63] The Whigs did succeed in passing
a resolution which stated that the war had been "unneces-
sarily and unconstitutionally begun by the President of the
United States." [64] But that alone meant little or nothing.
On a resolution disclaiming the desire for any indemnity and
suggesting the withdrawal of United States troops from the
territory west of the Rio Grande, the Whig House by a majority of over three to one proclaimed its disapproval.[65] The
most that can be said is that the administration may have
been more cautious in its policy toward Mexico in view of
the opposition majority in the House. When it came to actual
obstruction of war activities, however, the House of Representatives did not do anything. And it was the continuance
of the war that threatened the existence of Mexico. The Whig
oratory about the President's guilt in precipitating the conflict accomplished nothing in the direction of peace. There
is some evidence to show that Whig speeches tended to pro-
long the war by making it appear to the Mexicans that sacri-
fices of territory might ultimately not be necessary.[66]

Within a week after the assembling of Congress the absorption of Mexico became a topic of debate. The movement for
absorption had gained sufficient momentum to cause the
introduction of the question into the halls of the legislative
body. Certain members of Congress, including Calhoun, professed to believe that the measures recommended by Polk
were intended to provide for the acquisition of Mexico, or at
least that would be the result if the President's policies were
adopted.[67] While Polk's message was doubtless interpreted in

[63] Marcy to Wool, 18 November 1847, Marcy MSS. Private Letter
Book as Secretary of War.
[64] *Cong. Globe, 30th Cong., 1st sess.*, p. 95.
[65] *Ibid.*, pp. 93, 94.
[66] Trist to Buchanan, 20 December 1847, *30th Cong., 1st sess., S.
Doc. No. 52*, p. 270.
[67] Calhoun to A. P. Calhoun, 11 December 1847, *Correspondence of
Calhoun*, p. 741. See also statement of Representative Vinton,
Chairman of the Ways and Means Committee, *Cong. Globe, 30th
Cong., 1st sess.*, p. 102.

the light of preconceived opinions, it was not long until the question was presented in more concrete form. On December 14, Dickinson, of New York, a Hunker Democrat, offered resolutions in the Senate stating that " true policy requires the Government of the United States to strengthen its political and commercical relations upon this continent by the annexation of such contiguous territory as may conduce to that end, and can be justly obtained. . . ." [68] A principle which could be used to justify the annexation of the whole Western Hemisphere was contained in the New York senator's resolutions. Manifestations of public opinion formed the background, while Polk's message and Dickinson's resolutions furnished the immediate occasion for a struggle in Congress which was to end only with the treaty of peace.

Although the Whigs continued their clamor against Democratic imperialism, the leadership in the fight against the absorption of Mexico fell not to Whigs but to anti-slavery and pro-slavery Democrats. On December 20, Senator John M. Niles, of Connecticut, delivered a warning to the Senate. While believing it to be the general sentiment of the Senate that the conquest of Mexico was not to be desired, Niles confessed that he was afraid that the legislators might be " thrown into a position in which such a result will become almost inevitable." The farther the army advanced, according to the Senator from Connecticut, the more difficult would become the task of making peace. Already it was the belief of the army, of many members of the diplomatic service, and others that peace could not be made without the subjugation of all Mexico. Niles intimated that it was high time for the Senate " to view matters carefully, and to proceed with caution." [69] This was undoubtedly true. However, just a month later Niles, himself, seemed to be willing to fall in line with those who were demanding the annexation of Mexico.[70]

But it was pro-salvery Calhoun who stood out as the leading anti-imperialist in Congress and perhaps in the country.

[68] *Cong. Globe, 30th Cong., 1st sess.*, p. 21.
[69] *Ibid.*, p. 55.
[70] Niles to Van Buren, 20 January 1848, Van Buren MSS.

The Carolinian had been in favor of Polk's scheme to acquire Upper California and New Mexico just before the outbreak of war.[71] The slavery agitation, however, had brought Calhoun to the point where he would have apparently been glad to adopt the " no territory " platform of the Whigs had such a course appeared feasible.[72] The day after Dickinson's effort Calhoun introduced resolutions protesting against the conquest of Mexico, to be held either as a province or incorporated in the Union. This would be, he said, " in the end, subversive of our free and popular institutions." [73] On numerous occasions Calhoun warned the Senate against the " evil " and " hazard " involved in the absorption of Mexico.[74] After one of his speeches on the subject the New York *Herald,* one of the most outspoken expansionist organs in the country, declared that the Carolinian's remarks had produced a " bombshell in every quarter." Many of Henry Clay's supporters said that they would be just as willing to vote for Calhoun. " If any man," continued the *Herald,* " can produce a change or revolution in the public mind in the North, it is now acknowledged that Mr. Calhoun is that personage, and all admit that he has taken the wind out of the sails of Clay, Webster, and all other orators of the day." [75] The expansionists in Congress feared the opposition of Calhoun more than that coming from any other quarter for most of

---

[71] Polk's *Diary,* I, 317.

[72] Calhoun to Thompson, 29 October 1847, *Correspondence of Calhoun,* p. 738. It should be pointed out that Calhoun was not on very friendly terms with the Polk administration. The South Carolinian was somewhat disgruntled because he was not retained in the cabinet. Calhoun to Hunter, 26 March 1845, Charles H. Ambler, ed., *Correspondence of Robert M. T. Hunter, 1826-1876,* in *Annual Report of the American Historical Association for 1916,* II, 76. Then, too, Calhoun saw fit to oppose Polk's policy as regards both Oregon and Mexico. *Correspondence of Calhoun,* pp. 653, 689-691. As Calhoun probably thought that Polk intended to acquire all Mexico, it is legitimate to suspect that partisanship was not without effect. But it seems certain that the Carolinian believed that he was acting for the best interests of the South, perhaps of the Union, in opposing the absorption of Mexico.

[73] *Cong. Globe, 30th Cong., 1st sess.,* p. 26.

[74] *Ibid.,* pp. 26, 53-54, 96-97.

[75] New York *Herald,* 6 January 1848.

them addressed their remarks directly or indirectly to the
" Senator from South Carolina." [76]

If words meant anything, it would seem that during the
first three weeks of the session the expansionists in the Senate
had nothing but ridicule for the idea that all Mexico might
be annexed. According to Cass, of Michigan, " there is no
man in this nation in favor of the extinction of the nationality
of Mexico." [77] Senator Allen, of Ohio, a political supporter
of Cass, asserted that " there would be few opinions antago-
nistic " to Calhoun's on the subject of the absorption of
Mexico.[78] No one had said in the Senate that there was any
great demand for the absorption of Mexico. The question
was whether or not it could be prevented if the fighting continued much longer. The trouble was that the amount of
popular support for the absorption of Mexico could not be
definitely ascertained in December, 1847. A presidential campaign was due in a few months. Why should Cass, who was
destined to win the Democratic nomination, make a prema-
ture declaration on the subject? It would be much better to
let one's attitude toward perplexing questions be disclosed as
public sentiment became easier to measure.[79] The opinion of
the public, and that of Cass along with it, developed rapidly.
Just ten days after he had declared that nobody wanted to
absorb Mexico the Michigan Senator concluded that " to
attempt to prevent the American people from taking possession of Mexico, if they demand it, would be as futile in
effect, as to undertake to stop the rushing of the cataract of
Niagara." It took Cass less than two weeks to discover the

---

[76] For remarks of Allen, Westcott, Davis, of Mississippi, Stanton
and Cass, see *Cong. Globe, 30th Cong., 1st sess.*, pp. 54, 90, 92-93,
135, 216.

[77] *Ibid.*, p. 54.   [78] *Ibid.*

[79] On January 2, 1848, Nugent, alias Galviensis, the Washington
Correspondent of the New York *Herald*, commented on the attitude of
the Senate: " Senators on both sides of the chamber have expressed
their belief that nobody in the United States contemplates the annexation of the whole of Mexico. This is a great mistake. Everybody in the United States has been weighing the question, and the
Senators themselves have been speculating upon it in its political
aspect. . . . This may be deemed *scandalum magnatum*; but it is,
nevertheless, true." New York *Herald*, 6 January 1848.

fact that "the more the war is prolonged . . . the greater will be the danger of such an occurrence. . . ." [80] Whether the politicians liked it or not they would soon have to take a definite stand either for or against the absorption of Mexico if peace did not come.

Meanwhile the question of the absorption of Mexico had been introduced into the House. On the same day that Calhoun offered his resolutions in the Senate, Holmes, also a Democrat of South Carolina, presented like sentiments to the House.[81] Expressions of opposition to the dismemberment of Mexico came from several northern and southern Whigs.[82] It was Richardson, an Illinois Democrat, who was the first to take up the cudgels for the expansionists. He stated that the United States must have indemnity for the war and "the amount of the indemnity must necessarily depend upon the obstinacy of the enemy and the duration of the war." [83] As the enemy appeared to be fairly obstinate and the war did not seem to be nearing its end, Richardson may be listed with those who were willing to take all Mexico. At any rate, by the end of December the annexation of Mexico had become a subject for debate in the House as well as in the Senate. Just what members were in favor of absorption and what members were against it would be disclosed during the debates of January and February, 1848.

It appears, then, that in the period from October through December, 1847, the annexation or the absorption by some means or another of all Mexico, became a topic of general interest in the United States. In the press, in the administration, in Congress and among army officers one can notice the emergence of a widespread belief that peace could be established only by the extinction of Mexican independence. This was not always clearly expressed, and there were even yet relatively few who frankly favored the absorption of the

---

[80] *Cong. Globe, 30th Cong., 1st sess.*, p. 79.
[81] *Ibid.*, p. 38.
[82] For resolutions of Botts, of Virginia, Stephens, of Georgia, Vandyke, of New Jersey, and Thompson, of Indiana, see *ibid.*, pp. 61-62.
[83] *Ibid.*, p. 59.

southern republic. Until the beginning of 1848, so far as
Congress and the politicians were concerned, the opponents
of annexation took the center of the stage. Those who would
later be identified with the movement, for the most part
either kept silent or issued denials and Delphic utterances.
They were waiting on public opinion. Nevertheless, it may
safely be said that in the fall and early winter of 1847 the
possibility of the absorption of Mexico appeared obvious to
almost everybody; the probability of such an occurrence
seemed likely to a less numerous body; while an even smaller
though increasing number of people would welcome Mexico
with open arms.

There were no sudden or startling developments in the
movement for the absorption of Mexico which differentiated
the last three months of 1847 from the first two months of
1848. Changes noted will be marked by differences more of
degree rather than of kind. The later part of 1847 saw the
definite emergence of the issue, while January and February,
1848, witnessed the sentiment for all Mexico at its period of
greatest strength. The presidential campaign of 1848 was
drawing nearer and nearer. It was obvious that the Mexican
question, barring unexpected developments, would be the
dominant issue of the campaign. Consequently parties and
candidates would be forced to take a more or less definite
stand. A politician casting his eyes over the scene in 1848
was likely to be convinced that the party and candidate who
took the most vigorous attitude toward Mexico would win in
the approaching contest. He would doubtless have been correct had not events removed the question from the domain of
politics some two months later. Congress was in continuous
session from December 7 until the end of the war, and the
debates and maneuvers of politicians kept the subject constantly before the people. Comments in the press on the proceedings in Congress and on the probable outcome of the war
added fuel to the flame. Public irritation and impatience had
not been diminished by the futile efforts to make peace with
Mexico, but on the other hand were constantly increasing.

These are some of the reasons why the drive for annexation began to take on new aspects in 1848.

The increasing expansionist sentiment manifested itself in various ways. There was the appearance of a tendency to advocate the absorption of Mexico as the best possible solution of the problem created by the war, and not merely because it seemed to be the only way out of the difficulty. Motives appealing to the idealist, the materialist and the nationalist were supplied, world without end, to justify the extinction of Mexican independence. In Congress and in the administration, expansionist politicians began to reveal their ideas with less camouflage. There was still, however, sufficient ambiguity and contradiction in the statements coming from the representatives of the people. A further breakdown in the Whig opposition to the war and territorial indemnity and the beginning of an abolitionist drive for all Mexico could also be noted. In fact, there were expressions of opinion to the effect that the greatest opposition to the absorption of Mexico would come from eastern slaveholders, especially from South Carolina and her great leader, Calhoun. It was with developments of this type that the movement for the absorption of Mexico proceeded to its conclusion in the early months of 1848.

The presidential campaign was inaugurated, so far as the Democrats were concerned, by a series of political gatherings in which the absorption of Mexico, or what amounted to that, was the chief topic of discussion. At a public dinner given in his honor at Philadelphia on December 30, Commodore Stockton delivered what *Niles' Register* called "the most striking and direct to the purpose" of all speeches regarding the conquest of Mexico.[84] As for that benighted country, Stockton would "forgive all her trespasses, and returning good for evil, make her free and happy." The United States had "a duty before God which we cannot—we must not evade." Stockton would carry on the war for fifty years if necessary for the "express purpose of redeeming Mexico from

---

[84] *Niles' Register*, LXXIII, 334.

misrule and civil strife." " I would with a magnanimous and kindly hand," declared the Commodore, " gather these wretched people within the fold of republicanism. . . . This I would accomplish at any cost." [85] This speech, breathing the spirit of Holy Writ, was followed by others at a banquet held in Washington early in January. Vice-President Dallas, Senators Dickinson and Cass and General Shields were among the notables present. After dwelling on the " splendid destiny " which the future had in store for his country, Dickinson offered a toast: " A more perfect Union: embracing the entire North American continent." Replying to another toast, Shields was willing to admit that there was some " talent and ability" among his Whig friends, but they had been " warring against destiny. . . ." [86] There was concealed within all this high-flown verbiage an earnest desire to present the absorption of Mexico in as attractive a form as possible to the public.

Meetings of this general character followed each other in rapid succession throughout January. General Pierce, with implied approval of the *puro* program, told a New Hampshire audience that this Mexican party would insist on keeping the Americans in Mexico in order to preserve their freedom and political rights.[87] New York Democrats were especially active in the drive for all Mexico. On January 6, a call was issued to all those " who wish to hold on to military glory and the mines of all Mexico at any expense," to attend a meeting for the purpose of furthering that policy.[88] Three weeks later the New York Hunker Democratic convention undertook to prove by means of resolutions that a legal title to Mexico could be secured by conquest.[89] On January 29, a mass meeting was held at Tammany Hall. Those ardent expansionists, Senators Foote, of Mississippi, and Houston, of Texas, were imported to make the principal speeches.

---

[85] *Ibid.*, p. 335.   [86] *Ibid.*, p. 336.
[87] Boston *Post*, 27 January 1848. The *puros* were a radical republican group many of whom desired annexation to the United States. Rives, *The United States and Mexico*, II, 590-592; Smith, II, 233-236.
[88] New York *Herald*, 6 January 1848.
[89] *Niles' Register*, LXXIII, 391; Dodd, p. 164.

Foote explained to the New York Democrats that he was not quite prepared for annexation, but it was "our duty before God to protect the people of Mexico." The Mexican people desired this protection and if the United States refused, England would take charge of the business. The Mississippian did not deem it necessary to dwell upon the ultimate effect of "protecting" the Mexicans. Why complicate the issue by raising such extraneous questions? Manifest destiny was the theme of Houston's address. "The Americans regard this continent as their birthright," declared the Texan. Nothing could stop the Anglo-Saxons who were destined "to pervade the whole Southern extremity of this vast continent." Houston did not fail to intimate to his audience that they now had a good opportunity to take Mexico and that the process might not be without its pleasant side.

I would [said he] recommend you, if the country should be acquired, to take a trip of exploration there, and look out for the beautiful *senoritas*, or pretty girls, and if you choose to annex them, no doubt the result of this annexation will be a most powerful and delightful evidence of civilization.

After hearing these representatives from the Southwest, the New Yorkers resolved "That the indefinite extension of our territory, and the spread of our free institutions has nothing in it alarming to our minds." [90] The arguments of Houston and Foote apparently did not fall on deaf ears.

These maneuvers showed that Democratic politicians, many of whom were in favor of expansion for its own sake, were convinced that public opinion could be led to support a program providing, at least indirectly, for the absorption of Mexico. At the same time, the speeches of Stockton, Dickinson, Shields, Foote and Houston furnish an interesting study of the psychology of American politics and imperialism. The political campaign assumed the character of a religious revival with its reliance on an appeal to the emotions. For the idealist and the religiously minded, it was declared that the United States had a "duty before God" to rescue the Mexicans from their state of degradation. This, so it was said,

---

[90] New York *Herald*, 30 January 1848.

was the ardent desire of the better classes in Mexico and was
a predestined event whatever might be the intentions of mor-
tals. To appeal to the nationalist, pictures of the glory of a
far-flung republic and the threat of European intervention
were pressed into service. The " mines of all Mexico " could
be counted on to draw the attention of capitalist interests.
Would the American people be able to resist the appeal to
their idealism, their patriotism, their greed and their innate
desire to expand? It was at best exceedingly doubtful.

Nor did it seem that the politicians were wrong in their
interpretation of the probable trend of public opinion. There
appears to have been a steady growth in January and February, 1848, of the sentiment for the absorption of Mexico.
This received recognition from enemies as well as friends.
In the East, and especially in New York, expansionism waxed
strong. Leading organs of public opinion directly or by
implication advocated the absorption of Mexico.[91] Numerous articles advocating annexation, said *Niles' Register*,
" are gracing journals published in this free, this enlight-
ened, this *christian* country—this *model republic.*" [92] Governor Briggs, of Massachusetts, apparently thinking that Mexico was about to lose her nationality, concluded that the

---

[91] For examples, see Boston *Post*, 1 February 1848; New York
Herald, 26 January 1848; New York *Evening Post*, quoted by *Niles'
Register*, LXXIII, 334; *Democratic Review*, XXII, 279.

[92] *Niles' Register*, LXXIII, 334. The movement for annexation
received attention from would-be humorists. As one wag declared:
" The high pressure steamer Annexation, Capt. Polk, master, Gen.
Cass, mate, and R. J. Walker, clerk, will leave the mouth of the Rio
Grande on the fourth of July, touching at Tampico, Vera Cruz, the
Halls of the Montezumas, and other places in Mexico, thence via
Central America, through the South American States on the Pacific
side, returning around Cape Horn and touching at all the interme-
diate ports . . . thence she will proceed to all and several of the
West India Islands, whence she will return to Washington, where she
will be dismantled and sold out for the benefit of the underwriters.
For freight and passage apply to General Cass. Negroes (ranking
as citizens) will be taken on board South of the Rio Grande, but on
the return trip they will be left at Hayti.
" N. B. Capt. Taylor, with his submarine apparatus and caout-
chouc camels, will accompany the steamer, to lift her over the bars.
Gentlemen having money to lend will apply to the clerk." New
York *Herald*, 31 January 1848.

results would be " far more appalling than the war itself." [93]
A New York Whig wrote at the end of January that " it
appears now, that the people are quite willing, to sanction
the taking of *all Mexico,* and holding it too." [94] " . . . the
American mind is not made up fully in favor of annexation," said the *Democratic Review,* " yet it leans that way." [95]
By February 9, the New York *Herald* thought there would
soon be presented a project in Congress calling for a national
convention to draw up a new form of government for such a
republic as would be formed by Mexico and the United
States.[96] Verily, the imperialists were advancing rapidly in
their march on the " Halls of the Montezumas."

And what were the motives of the eastern expansionists?
One may be sure that they were many and various. Doubtless many were convinced that it was indeed the destiny of
the United States to take and civilize Mexico; and the Mexican War furnished a fine opportunity to fulfill that mission.
Others felt that there was no other way to bring the war to a
satisfactory conclusion.[97] Still others, among them a former
cabinet officer, thought that whatever was left of Mexico after
the war would immediately become an object of European
interference.[98] The obvious thing to do was to leave none of
Mexico to become a prey to foreign powers. But there were

---

[93] *Niles' Register,* LXXIII, 334.
[94] Mower to McLean, 24 January 1848, McLean MSS.
[95] *Democratic Review,* XXII, 279.
[96] New York *Herald,* 9 February 1848.
[97] New York *Evening Post,* quoted by *Niles' Register,* LXXIII,
334; New York *Herald,* 5 January 1848. In a speech in the Senate
on January 11, Reverdy Johnson, of Maryland, stated: " I have
heard it said by some that this war should be prosecuted because its
tendency was to ameliorate the condition of Mexico. I have heard it
said that we were constituted missionaries by Heaven, even by fire
and by sword, to carry the light of civilization into that benighted
land. I have heard that it has been stated even in the pulpit that
we have been selected by Divine Providence to purify a dark and
false religion . . . to bring them into the blaze of the true faith,
and to substitute for it the holier and purer light of the Protestant
religion. I have heard it stated, Mr. President, that this war is to
be prosecuted in order to enlarge 'the area of freedom! ' . . ."
Cong. Globe, 30th Cong., 1st sess., p. 149.
[98] Louis McLane to Calhoun, 18 January 1848, *Correspondence
Addressed to Calhoun,* p. 425.

other and more sordid motives. Financial, commercial and industrial groups were interested in securing extensive additions of territory because it was thought this would stimulate enterprise, strengthen the United States in the markets of Europe, and result in a high tariff policy.[99] Moreover, the rich lands and mines of Mexico could be used to " pay every expense of the war, so as to save the revulsion of the banks, by a continuation of the war by taxes and loans in this country." [100] For one reason or another the absorption of Mexico appeared attractive to certain elements in the Northeast. But a conviction that Mexico would never agree to an honorable peace and an appreciation of the economic advantages to be derived from annexation were probably the most influential factors in the eastern annexationist movement.

A survey of public opinion in the Southeast in January and February, 1848, reveals the same tendency, already noted, to view with alarm current trends toward the absorption of Mexico. In his opposition to the acquisition of Mexico Calhoun reflected the sentiments of most of the leaders of the slavocracy. In the press there were expressions of dire foreboding that either peace or annexation in some form must come in the near future.[101] " I should not be surprised," said a writer in the Charleston *Courier,* " before the expiration of three months to see those who doubt . . . [the expedience of conquering and holding Mexico] denounced as guilty of moral treason. . . ." [102] Many southern Democrats, as well as Whigs, continued to deplore the apparent probability of the conquest of Mexico. Said Gadsden, of South Carolina:

The great object at this time is to arrest the mad designs of Conquest; involving the still more dreaded but unavoidable policy, if the first succeeds, of the Annexation of the whole of Mexico, in states to the Union. I can not reflect on the measure without the most

[99] Hatcher to Calhoun, 5 January 1848, and Winslow to Calhoun, 1 February 1848, *ibid.,* pp. 418-419, 428-429.
[100] New York *Herald,* 7 January 1848.
[101] *Southern Quarterly Review,* XIII, 236-237; *Charleston Mercury,* 17 January 1848.
[102] Article signed " Lowndes " in Charleston *Courier,* quoted by *Niles' Register,* LXXIII, 354.

fearful apprehensions for the character and security of this Government or Confederation.[103]

Calhoun's correspondence contains many letters of the same general tenor.[104] Pro-slavery Democrats and Whigs gave many reasons for opposing the acquisition of Mexico. In addition to charges that conquest was immoral and unjust, it was alleged that the absorption of large numbers of ignorant Mexicans would weaken or destroy American institutions. Then too, it was said that England and France might intervene, especially if the United States did not assume the Mexican debt of 100 millions. It was contended that Mexico was not worth this much and indeed was not worth what it would cost to conquer her. All this was doubtless no more than a rationalization of the most important motives for southern opposition which came from a fear of the sectional issue over slavery and from a conviction that all Mexico would come into the Union as free territory.[105]

Perhaps the case of John A. Campbell, of Alabama, will illustrate the mental reaction which was taking place in the minds of many southern Democrats, although few followed Campbell in giving such frank expression to their views.

---

[103] J. Gadsden to Calhoun, 23 January 1848, *Correspondence Addressed to Calhoun*, pp. 425-426.

[104] *Correspondence of Calhoun*, pp. 1135, 1140, 1149-1150; *Correspondence Addressed to Calhoun*, pp. 408, 412, 419, 420, 421, 427, 429.

[105] *Ibid.* See also Charleston *Mercury*, 30 December 1847; speech of Governor Johnson of South Carolina, *ibid.*, 23 November 1847; Cole, *The Whig Party in the South*, pp. 122-123; Boucher, *In Re that Aggressive Slavocracy*, pp. 33-42. Perhaps another reason for southern opposition to absorption was the fact that in anti-slavery quarters there was beginning a movement in favor of extensive annexations. Although the rumor was probably untrue, it was reported that the venerable John Quincy Adams favored the absorption of Mexico. New York *Herald*, 3 January 1848. When this report reached South Carolina the editor of the most widely-read newspaper in the state exclaimed: "When John Quincy Adams advocates the incorporation of Mexico, either in whole or in part, we may be sure that our interest and safety are not certainly to be promoted. *We know what we are; we know not what we may be!*" Charleston *Mercury*, 17 January 1848. If the anti-slavery forces were about to begin the trek to Mexico, it certainly behooved the South to draw back.

During the Mexican War Campbell was practicing law in
Alabama. He later became an associate justice of the Supreme
Court and was one of the majority which handed down the
Dred Scott decision. Campbell frankly regarded the " acquisition of New Territory mainly as it may affect the *balance*
of power in the federal government." He thought that Mexican territory was " wholly unfit for a negro population," and
that all territory acquired from Mexico would result in an
" increase of the strength of the nonslaveholding states and
a corresponding dimunition of our own." Campbell also held
in March, 1848, that Congress had a legal right to prevent
slavery in the territories of the United States.[106] Holding
these views he very naturally declared that the South should
oppose the acquisition of any Mexican territory. As extensive conquests became increasingly likely, Campbell concluded
that " Mr. Polk's war . . . [was] likely to produce the most
disastrous consequences to the Southern States." " This
war," said he, " was not brought on by any act and I may
say any fault of Mexico. Our President invaded a territory
claimed by that Republic and over which its laws pre-
vailed." [107] A realization that the interests of the South
would be adversely affected by the acquisition of Mexican
territory had caused Campbell to take the position occupied
by the extreme anti-slavery Whigs as to the President's rôle
in producing the war.[108] Here was a concrete expression of

---

[106] A rather strange opinion from one who was later one of the
majority of the Supreme Court which declared that the Missouri
Compromise was unconstitutional.

[107] For a connected summary of Campbell's views, see his letters
to Calhoun, 20 November, 20 December 1847, *Correspondence of
Calhoun*, pp. 1139-1142, 1155; 1 March 1848, *Correspondence Addressed to Calhoun*, p. 431.

[108] This coming together of extremes was apparent in the case of
pro-slavery Calhoun and anti-slavery Hale, both of whom took
practically the same ground concerning the continuance of the
Mexican War, but for opposite reasons. One northern newspaper
carried an interesting editorial on Calhoun and Hale. New York
Herald, 7 January 1848. Massachusetts and South Carolina joined
hands when Governors Briggs and Johnson both opposed the annexation of Mexico. To Briggs, such a result of the war would be " far
more appalling that the war itself," while to Johnson, it would lead
to a contest " more disastrous than the war itself." *Niles' Register*,

a view which, in so far as it related to the acquisition of Mexican territory, was rapidly becoming widespread in the Southeast.

In the Southwest, however, sentiment for the absorption of Mexico marched blithely forward, obstructed little if at all by concern for the institution of slavery. While Houston was expatiating to a New York audience on the destiny of the Anglo-Saxon, Ashbel Smith, another prominent Texan, was telling the same story to a local audience.[109] The Texan legislature passed resolutions which scarcely concealed a desire to acquire all Mexico, or at least a greater portion of the country.[110] Governor Johnson's message to the Louisiana legislature in January was stamped with the same general character.[111] General John A. Quitman, of Mississippi, was " unable to perceive the very great evils to arise from adding to our confederacy one of the most beautiful and productive countries on the face of the earth. . . ."[112] The New Orleans *Picayune* denied that Calhoun's contentions as to the evil effects of the absorption of Mexico had any basis in fact. According to the editor, Cass, also, was wrong when he stated that no one had any idea of absorbing Mexico. " There is such a party in the United States and it is a growing one too, at that." [113]

It seems, therefore, that the eastern slavocracy could not count on western slaveholders for aid in fighting the movement for the absorption of Mexico. Not that the interests of slavery were overlooked in the Southwest; but so bound up was the western spirit with ideas of nationalism and manifest

---

LXXIII, 334; Charleston *Mercury*, 23 November 1847. It looks as though the two Governors might have compared notes before addressing their respective legislatures. On this point, if on nothing else, the pro-slavery and anti-slavery interests were in agreement; but it is by no means certain that slavery furnished the principal motivation for Massachusetts' opposition to absorption.

[109] Rippy, pp. 16-17.

[110] *Niles' Register*, LXXIII, 238; *Cong. Globe, 30th Cong., 1st sess.*, p. 410.

[111] New York *Herald*, 31 January 1848.

[112] Quitman to Knox, 8 March 1848, *Life and Correspondence of General Quitman*, II, 14.

[113] New Orleans *Picayune*, 31 December 1847.

destiny that it was a case, not of loving Caesar less, but Rome more. The West furnished some of the most uncompromising champions of slavery, but they were not disposed to miss the opportunity of seizing large areas or the whole of Mexico, and they had too much faith in American institutions to fear that the addition of eight million Mexicans could overthrow the Union. Nevertheless, when all is said and done, it seems certain that an overwhelming majority of slaveholders as a class were opposed to the absorption of Mexico. Among those slaveholders who were principally concerned with the fortunes of slavery, opposition was almost unanimous.[114]

All generalizations lay themselves open to criticism, but it is apparently safe to say that the free states of the West were, on the whole, more favorable to the absorption of Mexico than any other section of the Union. All the leading Democratic newspapers joined the drive for all Mexico.[115] The Michigan legislature was practically a unit in favor of acquiring the whole country.[116] True it is that the Detroit *Free Press,* following its idol, Lewis Cass, declared as late as February 11, that the " destruction of the national independence of Mexico was never thought of." [117] Yet this same paper had been constantly advocating a policy which amounted to practical absorption, and was one of the few journals which expressed dissatisfaction with the Treaty of Guadalupe Hidalgo because it did not secure enough territory.[118] Its denial of the existence of a demand for all Mexico was nothing but an assertion to the contrary. So popular was the war and annexation in Illinois that when Abraham Lincoln, a Whig member of Congress from that state, undertook to question the justice of the war and the policy of the administration he

---

[114] Dodd maintains that all the leading Democratic papers of the South and West supported the absorption of Mexico for a time. Dodd, p. 171. This seems to be true enough so far as the West is concerned. But a perusal of the files of such journals as the Richmond *Enquirer,* the Charleston *Mercury* and the Nashville *Union* fails to reveal at any time a demand for all Mexico.

[115] Dodd, p. 171.

[116] New York *Herald,* 13 January 1848.

[117] Detroit *Free Press,* 11 February 1848.

[118] *Ibid.,* 10 November 1847, 17 March 1848.

was denounced from one end of the state to the other. By his attitude on the Mexican question Lincoln destroyed whatever chance he had for reelection and the Whigs lost his constituency.[119] As will appear later, Illinois was the only state both of whose senators voted against the Treaty of Guadalupe Hidalgo because they desired more territory. One of the few men in Congress who advocated the absorption of Mexico without any equivocation whatever was Senator Sidney Breese, of Illinois. In fact, though they had allies in the East and in the South it was western Democratic members of Congress who formed the backbone of the expansionist movement. It cannot be supposed that they failed to represent the will of their constituents who worshipped the ideal of manifest destiny among their household gods.

The evidences of increased expansionist sentiment which appeared in all parts of the country in 1848, was not without influence in Whig circles. Reverdy Johnson informed the Senate that although he had opposed the policies of the Polk administration he now, in January, 1848, found himself differing from most of the Whigs on the Mexican question. Johnson avowed his intention of supporting a vigorous prosecution of the war " to have American rights recognized, and American honor vindicated; and so recognized and so vindicated, as to furnish full and complete security against subsequent violations." [120] This sounded much like a speech from some Democratic expansionist. Senator Johnson, of Louisiana, deemed it expedient to assure the members of the Louisiana legislature that he would vote supplies for the war and support a vigorous prosecution of hostilities.[121] No ex-

---

[119] Albert J. Beveridge, *Abraham Lincoln 1809-1858*, I, 422-433.

[120] *Cong. Globe, 30th Cong., 1st sess.*, pp. 137-140, 148. Johnson expressed the same sentiments at a dinner given in honor of Generals Quitman and Shields. Nashville *Union*, 12 January 1848. A Washington correspondent of the Boston *Post* declared that Johnson's speech in the Senate had angered the Clay Whigs, but had satisfied another wing of the party. Speaking of this latter group, the correspondent said: " Their policy is, ' d——n the administration, but carry on the war even to conquest.' And conquest they desire— they mean it, and, if possible will carry it out." Boston *Post*, 15 January 1848.

[121] Boston *Post*, 7 February 1848.

pansionist demanded more than that so far as the conduct of the war was concerned. The Whig Governor of New York in his message to the legislature expressed the most patriotic sentiments on the subject of the war and declared that an honorable peace would of necessity involve indemnity from Mexico.[122] On January 22, there appeared a notice in the New York *Herald* of a meeting of Taylor Whigs. The call to attend the gathering was addressed to all people of any party

who are in favor of the gradual absorption and annexation of all Mexico, on account of its great commercial advantages to the Northern States . . . [and] all who are anxious to prevent England, Spain, or any other nation of Europe, from taking possession of Mexico, and her gold and silver mines. . . .[123]

Even Secretary Walker would have found it difficult to criticize such a program.

This change in the attitude of some of the Whigs was but a continuation of the same process which had been going on since October, 1847. Increasing numbers of the party were becoming convinced that their political future would be endangered if they did not change their attitude toward the war and territorial indemnity from Mexico. Especially significant was the attitude of some of the Taylor Whigs. It apparently seemed to them that a platform calling for the absorption of Mexico with her mines of gold and silver would insure the election of their hero. The *National Whig* had already proposed such a program and now other Whigs were doing likewise. Given the information available in January, 1848, their tactics do not appear to have been unreasonable. The demand of some of the Whigs for territorial indemnity, and occasionally for all Mexico, furnishes the best of evidence of a belief that the voters were travelling in the same direction. Most of the Whig leaders, however, continued to voice their opposition to the war and to the acquisition of Mexican territory; but with not quite so much vigor as in 1846 and

---

[122] New York *Herald*, 5 January 1848; Richmond *Enquirer*, 7 January 1848.

[123] New York *Herald*, 22 January 1848.

the first half of 1847. It is perhaps lucky for them that hostilities ceased before the next election.

The last stages of the movement for the absorption of Mexico brought forth developments which were of even more significance than defections from Whig ranks. These developments had to do with slaveholders and abolitionists; on the one hand, there appeared evidences that the expansionists were beginning to realize that some of the most vigorous opposition to the acquisition of all Mexico, or indeed to the acquisition of any Mexican territory, would come from slaveholders; on the other hand, there can be noted the beginnings of an abolitionist drive for extensive annexations—the more the better. Far from being a war to extend slavery, it seemed that, given time, the struggle with Mexico might take on the characteristics of a crusade to weaken that institution. In so far as this was true, the actions of slaveholders and abolitionists were based on a common belief that no territory secured from Mexico would be open to slavery. The propaganda of 1847 to this effect began to bear fruit during the last three months of the war.

The opposition of Southeastern slaveholders to the annexation of all Mexico has already been treated. As time went on the expansionists began to take note of this pro-slavery obstacle in their path, especially after Calhoun introduced his resolutions in the Senate protesting against the wholesale acquisition of Mexican territory. "Mr. C., with a great portion of the slave influence," said the Illinois *Globe*, "have no doubt, determined to oppose the extension of our borders. Our country is coming to a pretty pass between the Abolition Wilmot humbuggers and the slaveholders of the South." [124] The Washington correspondent of the New York *Herald* wrote that the most serious opposition to the annexation of all Mexico would come from South Carolina.[125] The antislavery *National Era* noted with apparent satisfaction the opposition of Whig slaveholders. "The policy of the annexa-

---

[124] Illinois *Globe*, quoted by the Illinois *State Register*, 31 December 1847.

[125] New York *Herald*, 6 January 1848.

tion of the whole of Mexico," said the editor, "is regarded as a most formidable Anti-Slavery measure." [126] A short time later the *National Era* informed its readers that Calhoun regarded the annexation of Mexico "as the deadliest blow that could be inflicted upon the system of slavery." [127] As will shortly appear, the *National Era* agreed with southern slaveholders as to the anti-slavery implications of the acqui-sition of Mexico. Senator J. M. Niles, anti-slavery Democrat of Connecticut, thought that every Democrat in the Senate except Calhoun and his friends would favor the removal of Mexico from the list of independent nations. Niles did not even except himself from the number but stated that he and Dix would "undoubtedly fall in with the scheme and go along with the current." [128] There is little evidence here of a belief in a pro-slavery expansion movement. On the con-trary, there seems to have been a feeling that a pro-slavery "conspiracy" against expansion was developing. In fact a northern clergyman called on Calhoun, "the highest embodi-ment of the principle involved in the domestic institutions of the South,"[129] to save the country from the effects of an anti-slavery crusade to annex Mexico.[130]

The truth is that the common myth of a pro-slavery drive for Mexican territory is based on evidence drawn largely from anti-slavery Whig sources. Anti-slavery expansionists were apparently not convinced that there was any diabolical scheme on the part of slaveholders to extend the area of slavery. Instead they realized that the opposition of some of the slaveholders was a most powerful obstacle to the absorp-tion of Mexico. It is true that such dyed-in-the-wool Whig anti-slavery champions as Giddings, Hale, Tuck, Palfrey, Sumner and their supporters persisted in their fight against the Mexican War because they said it was designed to extend

---

[126] *National Era*, 20 January 1848.
[127] *Ibid.*, 3 February 1848.
[128] Niles to Van Buren, 20 January 1848, Van Buren MSS.
[129] A characterization by the New York *Herald*, 7 January 1848.
[130] George H. Hatcher to Calhoun, 5 January 1848, *Correspondence Addressed to Calhoun*, p. 418.

slavery.[181] It may be that they took up the thesis of a " pro-slavery conspiracy " in order to enlist anti-slavery support in their attack on the war. There were of course many people who still thought that the acquisition of all Mexico might increase the power of the slavocracy and for that reason they were not in favor of expansion. But for the most part the charge that slaveholders were busily engaged in a war to promote the spread of slavery was advanced by anti-expansionists who happened at the same time to be opposed to slavery. It is not certain whether it was opposition, partisan or otherwise, to expansion or opposition to slavery which was more influential in determining the tactics of the Hale-Giddings-Sumner group. Be that as it may, it is not easy to give the anti-slavery Whigs credit for a great amount of sincerity when they accused slaveholders as a group of complicity in a scheme to add slaveholding territory to the Union. There was too much available evidence to the contrary.

And there is some reason for believing that northern Whigs were not so concerned about slave territory as appearances would indicate. No man was more extreme in his protests against the extension of slavery than was Joshua R. Giddings, of Ohio. Giddings seems to have thought that nothing could put a stop to conquests in Mexico. His chief concern, however, appears to have been not the slavery problem but the fact that if the Whig party became identified with the supporters of the war it would mean political disaster.[132] It is

---

[181] *Cong. Globe, 30th Cong., 1st sess.*, pp. 200, 245, 342, 394. John P. Hale, of New Hampshire, had Democratic antecedents, but his attitude toward the Mexican War was essentially the same as that of the northern Whigs. In fact Hale was looked upon as a Whig in certain quarters at the South. Charleston *Mercury*, 24 June 1847.

Salmon P. Chase, who had apparently secured his knowledge of the slavocracy from Charles Sumner, was somewhat astonished to find that all the slaveholders did not support the war. On the subject of a pro-slavery speech against the war, Chase wrote Sumner commenting on the strangeness of the occurrence. E. G. Bourne, *The Diary and Correspondence of Salmon P. Chase*, in *Annual Report of the American Historical Association for 1902*, II, 127. It would be interesting to know how Sumner replied to Chase. Opposition to the war on the part of slaveholders was certainly not in harmony with his thesis of war guilt.

[132] Giddings to Horace Greeley, 7 September 1847, George W.

possible that Giddings used the slavery club to hold northern Whigs in the straight and narrow path that would lead to political safety. Senator John M. Clayton, of Delaware, declared on the floor of the Senate that if all Mexico were annexed slavery would be " voted down " as a result.[133] Although Clayton represented a slave state he was identified with the northern Whig element. And the northern Whigs would have been glad to have seen slavery " voted down "; but they disliked Democratic expansion more than slavery.

Nor can the opposition of New England to extensive annexations be attributed entirely to slavery. That Whig champion, Daniel Webster, asserted in September, 1847, that " even if new acquired territory should be free territory, I should depreciate any great extension of our dominions." [134] It is a well-known fact that one of the chief arguments in Webster's famous speech, March 7, 1850, in favor of the compromise of 1850 was based on his assumption that slavery could not exist in the territory which had been taken from Mexico. Since Webster probably knew or suspected this in 1848, his opposition to westward extension was based on other grounds than slavery. There were other New Englanders who opposed extensive annexations, not so much on account of the slavery issue but because they believed that as the United States became larger New England would become relatively less important.[135] Holding these views they could scarcely be expected to approve expansion in any quarter.

Julian, *The Life of Joshua R. Giddings*, pp. 215-216. Some northern Whigs became disgusted with Giddings' oratory on the subject of slavery. One of them wrote Judge McLean: " I see your crazy old man Giddings is out in the western part of New York lecturing to the people, on Abolition and the extending of Slavery, in any new admitted territory. The man wants a straight jacket. He is ' negro crazy.' " Mower to McLean, 30 August 1847, McLean MSS. The writer of this letter, listening intently to the voice of the people, had about reached the conclusion that advocacy of expansion and political success went hand in hand. Above, pp. 90, 110. If Giddings were placed in a straight jacket the Whigs might be able to forget their pronouncements regarding slave territory and capitalize on the expansionist fever.

[133] *Cong. Globe, 30th Cong., 1st sess.*, p. 162.
[134] *Niles' Register*, LXXIII, 106.
[135] The gradual evolution of a certain section of New England

As a further illustration of the belief that the interests of slavery and expansion were not identical, there appeared early in 1848 an incipient demand for all Mexico from anti-slavery sources. Speaking of the annexation of all Mexico, the Washington correspondent of the New York *Herald* wrote: " The abolitionists will scarcely offer it a serious opposition. Mexico will all be free, and consequently the North will have no interest in opposing her annexation." [136]   On January 5, George Hatcher, a northern clergyman, described to Calhoun the situation as he saw it in the ranks of the anti-slavery forces:

From what I can gather I think I am safe in asserting that the project of an extensive acquisition of Mexican Territory is fast gaining ground among anti-Slavery men at the North. Familiar as I am with political and religious factions at the North I was not a little surprised to see how rapidly this idea is making a favorable lodgement in the public mind. . . . I refer now not simply to nominal Abolitionists but to that large portion of anti-Slavery men at the North who do not belong to Abolition organizations technically so called. It is this class of men and to the South the most formidable class who are fast becoming converts to the idea of *extensive annexation.* In their view the *more extensive the better.* Whether Slavery be extended over this territory or not they think its annexation will ultimately overthrow the institution. Mind you, however, they connect this effect with *extensive annexation.* They are coming to adopt this ground—' Territory without slavery *if they can,* but *with it rather than not have the territory.'* On the sup-

---

opinion can be traced in the *New Englander.* This journal declared when the war began that it had been brought on by the machinations of the slave power. A year later, however, the editor asserted that slaveholders had nothing to gain by annexing Mexican territory. Still the *New Englander* continued to deplore the probability of extensive territorial conquests. Some inkling of the reason for this attitude came after the war. Then the editor informed his readers, with implied disapproval, that as a result of the war Texas was to be the greatest and most powerful state in the Union. Several months later came the pronouncement that " smallness of territory has much to do with the strength of national attachments." It was " madness to think of comprehending in one country all that lies between the two oceans, and of bringing the whole of North America within the federal Union." If such a mania were to rule the hour it would be more desirable that the Pacific Ocean should lie just west of the Alleghanies. *New Englander,* IV, 432; V, 317-318, 604-605, 613; VI, 292-294, 587-588. It was this jealousy of her position in the Union that motivated to a great extent the anti-expansionist attitude of New England.
[136] New York *Herald,* 6 January 1848.

position that large territory be acquired and slavery extended over it they reason thus: 'In proportion as you extend slavery over a greater area in that proportion you weaken it.'

Hatcher then went on to explain exactly why the abolitionists thought extensive annexations would weaken slavery even though the institution were not kept out of the new territory.[137] While the writer undoubtedly exaggerated a tendency which appeared to him so dangerous to the safety of the Union, there was a certain amount of truth in his statements. Indeed it would have been very strange had not some of the abolitionists become convinced that expansion was inimicable to slavery. They had certainly heard many pronouncements to that effect from both slaveholders and non-slaveholders.

Much more important as evidence of the beginning of an anti-slavery demand for all Mexico was an editorial in the *National Era* of February 3, the substance of which was as follows; six months earlier the *National Era* had proposed a tentative plan for the union of Mexico and the United States; what had then appeared extravagant was now "seriously entertained by many sober, reflecting minds"; the change in public sentiment had induced Calhoun to warn his southern friends that the acquisition of Mexico would be disastrous in its effects on slavery; annexation would perhaps not disturb slavery in its present haunts, but would "erect a perpetual bar to its extension"; this was because Mexico would come into the Union as free territory, being unsuited to slave labor and already thickly populated with a people hostile to slavery. "With such views," continued the editor, "we must be pardoned for dwelling with pleasure upon the extension of our territory and the expansion of our population." [138]

This editorial registered a great change in the attitude of

---

[137] *Correspondence Addressed to Calhoun,* pp. 415-419. See also Boucher, p. 43 n. 47.

[138] *National Era,* 3 February 1848. The *National Era* was founded at Washington in January, 1847. The purpose of the paper was to urge the enforcement of the doctrines and measures characteristic of the Liberty party. According to the editor the *National Era* contemplated "no unconstitutional course no measures incompatible with the sovereignty of the States." *Ibid.,* 7 January 1847.

the *National Era*. The story as told by the editor during 1847 was the familiar one about the " pro-slavery conspiracy." In January, 1847, the " power and treasure of the republic " was being used for the extension of slave territory; in February, the extension of slave territory meant an increase in the strength of slavery since " slavery lives by expansion "; in April, Calhoun intended to make " the extension of slavery a great party issue, and himself the Presidential candidate of the South "; in October, the war had been " precipitated by the propagandists of slavery " and its termination by an honorable acquisition of territory was prevented " by their ruthless resolves to bring that territory under the blasting power of slavery." [139]   Between October, 1847, and the following February the theme of the story underwent considerable alteration. By the latter date, as noted above, the *National Era* was advocating the absorption of Mexico, insisting that it would be free territory, and citing along with other evidence, Calhoun's opposition to annexation as proof that the anti-slavery interests had nothing to fear from extensive territorial acquisitions. In other words, the *National Era* was convinced that if there had been a " pro-slavery conspiracy " to acquire all Mexico, it could not realize its ends even though the whole country were annexed. This conviction seems to have come largely as a result of the propaganda which was streaming from the northern expansionist press and the opposition of Calhoun. The editor probably reasoned that since Calhoun was opposing absorption the expansionists at the North must be correct. If the main body of the anti-slavery forces could be converted to this point of view, the movement for absorption which was growing rapidly at the time would doubtless become very strong indeed.

Care should be taken not to exaggerate the anti-slavery sentiment for all Mexico. It is evident that some such sentiment did exist, but there was not sufficient time for it to develop to significant proportions. The Treaty of Guadalupe Hidalgo had already been signed in Mexico when the

---

[139] *Ibid.*, 28 January, 4 February, 1 April, 7 October 1847.

National Era took up the cry of all Mexico on the grounds
that it would not be subject to slavery. In a short while the
war was over and whatever anti-slavery sentiment there was
for all Mexico collapsed along with the general expansion
movement. Had the war continued several months longer it
is not improbable that increasing numbers from the anti-
slavery camp would have joined forces with those who were
demanding the acquisition of Mexico. Their action would
have been based on the assumption that they were under-
mining the position of the pro-slavery forces. It was not to
be expected that those abolitionists, and there were undoubtedly some, who were using the bogey of "extension of
slavery" to cover up other reasons for opposition to annexation, would ever have become convinced of the error of their
ways. They would hold on to their pet theory to the bitter
end.

While public opinion seemed to be rapidly crystallizing in
favor of the absorption of Mexico, members of the administration, presumably in response to the trend of the popular
mind, also became somewhat more definite in their attitude
toward increased cessions of Mexican territory. On January
2, an interesting conversation took place between Polk and
Buchanan. The Secretary of State expressed himself as being
definitely in favor of taking Tamaulipas and all the country
east of the Sierra Madre Mountains. Buchanan gave as a
reason for his demand for additional territory the fact that
much money had been spent and many lives lost since Trist
had been given his instructions in April, 1847. The Secretary
might have added as another potent reason that he thought
the voters would favor increased cessions of territory. Polk
doubted the expediency of acquiring so large a number of
Mexicans but also declared that he, too, " would not now be
willing to agree to the terms " proposed in Trist's instructions.

I suggested [said Polk] that we might accede to a cession of New
Mexico, the Two Californias, & the passage across the Istmus [sic] of
Tehuantepec, paying for them a much less sum than Mr. Trist had
been authorized to offer, & that we should in addition secure the
port of Tampico. I told him [Buchanan] I would be glad to acquire

all the country he suggested, but that I apprehended that would not be practicable after the terms which Mr. Trist had already offered.[140]

It will be noted that Polk had reached the point where he would have been " glad " to take all the territory as far as the Sierra Madre range even though it would include large numbers of Mexicans, had not Trist's offer made this impracticable. Moreover, he had definitely determined to demand more than Upper California and New Mexico. One wonders how it happened that the President thought it might be practicable to get any increased territorial cessions with Mexican consent. So far as he knew at the time Mexico would not even agree to the terms offered by Trist. As it appeared later, Polk, himself thought it doubtful that Mexico would ever consent to give up more territory than the bare minimum which Trist had been authorized to accept.[141] What then would happen? This cannot be predicted with any degree of certainty; but it is probable that had Trist not taken the matter out of the hands of the Washington officials they would have been forced to take all Mexico or else moderate their demands.

And as January wore on it did not seem that moderation would be the order of the day. On the twelfth, Senator Rusk, of Texas, asked the President not to commit himself " further than I had done in my messages, against acquiring the whole of Mexico. . . ." In effect Polk agreed to Rusk's request.[142] It would seem that the senator from Texas was one of those who interpreted the messages as leaving the way open for the absorption of all Mexico. Walker was sick during most of December and January and did not take an active part in cabinet discussions but his views were well known. The Secretary of the Treasury was considered to be the real leader of those politicians who wanted to take Mexico.[143] Toward

---

[140] Polk's *Diary*, III, 277.

[141] *Ibid.*, pp. 347-348.

[142] " I told him that my views upon the first point [acquisition of Mexico] were distinctly stated in my messages, that I had not changed them, and [that I] left them to explain themselves." *Ibid.*, p. 298; Bourne, p. 498.

[143] Niles to Van Buren, 20 January 1848, Van Buren MSS; McCormac, p. 529 n. 88.

the end of January Walker was able to make public his
"gratifying belief that Mexico no longer exists as an independent nation, but will henceforth be associated with the
United States, forming a portion of the mighty republic of
the North." [144] This frankness is refreshing. The politician
had completely given way to the expansionist, or rather the
expansionist thought that it was now safe to come out into
the open.

Vice-President Dallas and Secretary Buchanan were rivals
for the support of the Democracy of Pennsylvania in the
coming presidential contest. They both made haste to issue
statements for publication which were political masterpieces.
The Secretary of State told Philadelphia Democrats that the
better class of Mexicans "dread nothing so much as the
withdrawal of our army." If all efforts to secure an honorable
peace should fail, "then we must fulfill that destiny which
Providence may have in store for both countries." [145] Buchanan was thus able to make public the exact words he had
tried to insert in the President's annual message. Pennsylvania voters must have been impressed with the noble sentiments of Dallas.

Let us not shrink from subjugating implacable enemies, when we
know that by so doing we shall advance the great objects of civilization. . . . Opposed as I am to receive permanently into the family
of American freemen those who are unwilling to enter it, I can yet
discover in our noble constitution of government nothing not perfectly equal to the vast task which may be assigned to it by the
resistless force of events—the guardianship of a crowded and con-
federated continent.[146]

So far as the administration was concerned the adherents
of the acquisition of all Mexico could rely on the Secretary
of the Treasury in any event; when the expansionists had
produced sufficient clamor they would find the Vice-President
and the Secretary of State in their front ranks; if events
did not soon lead to peace they might be able to secure the

---

[144] Boston *Post*, 3 February 1848.
[145] As quoted by Senator Bell, of Tennessee, *Cong. Globe, 30th
Cong., 1st sess.* (Appendix), p. 197; Bourne, p. 495 n. 1.
[146] *Niles' Register*, LXXIII, 392.

President who would probably be followed by the rest of the cabinet. Unfortunately for the designs of the expansionists, however, peace was almost at hand.

Not only were the revelations of expansionist sentiment producing an effect on members of the administration but even more unmistakable was the reaction in Congress to the signs of the times. During January and February most of the debate centered around the question of the probable effect on the fate of all Mexico of the measures proposed by the friends of the administration. Generally speaking the expansionists advocated the continuation of an offensive war while their opponents called for the occupation of a defensive line. Each side insisted that the policy of the other would lead to the absorption of Mexico. There was a third group composed of irreconcilable Whigs who demanded the withdrawal of United States troops from Mexico, but such a proposal had not sufficient support to bring it within the realm of possibility.[147] There seems to have been a realization on the part of both the friends and the enemies of expansion that as matters were the United States might be called on to take possession of the whole of the southern republic rather than merely California and New Mexico. Calhoun's resolutions had precipitated the issue and in January and February the debate went on, gathering momentum with the progress of time.

The opponents of absorption are not hard to locate. Almost all the Whig party took the view that an addition to the United States forces in Mexico, which meant a more vigorous prosecution of the war, would ultimately mean the end of Mexican independence.[148] Many members of the party contended that these measures recommended by the administration were expressly designed to effect the permanent sub-

---

[147] A resolution to that effect was defeated in the Whig House by a vote of 137 to 41. *Cong. Globe, 30th Cong., 1st sess.*, p. 94.

[148] As has been noted two Whig senators, Johnson, of Maryland, and Johnson, of Louisiana, supported a vigorous war against Mexico. But apparently the sentiment for absorption within Whig ranks had not yet gained sufficient strength to induce Whig members of Congress to demand extensive annexations of Mexican territory.

jugation of Mexico. Others, while not attributing to the President a definite scheme to acquire the whole country, insisted that if his recommendations were carried out absorption would be the inevitable result. Death to American institutions was the dire calamity which these Whigs asserted, with more or less sincerity, would follow the absorption of Mexico.[149]

Closely identified with the Whig opposition to absorption was the Calhoun wing of the Democrats.[150] There were other Democrats who had no desire to acquire Mexico,[151] but the chief opposition came from southeastern slaveholders. Calhoun, as we have seen, was regarded as the leader of the forces opposed to extensive annexations. He had been the first to voice his opposition in the Thirtieth Congress and thereafter most of the efforts of the expansionists were directed toward Calhoun's seat. The attitude of the Calhounites was somewhat similar to that of the Whigs, though they did not heap so much denunciation in public on the head of the President. In general the southeasterners were willing to acquire California and New Mexico,[152] but asserted that an offensive war would lead to the absorption of all Mexico. Like the Whigs they animadverted on the danger to American institutions involved in the acquisition of large numbers of Mexicans.[153] Again it should be emphasized that the slaveholding opponents of annexation did not lose sight of the fact that slavery was one of the institutions which might be adversely affected by a union with Mexico. It was a combination, then, composed of the majority of the Whig

[149] For statements of Senators Clayton, Mangum, Clarke and Bell, and Representatives Fisher and Crozier, see *Cong. Globe, 30th Cong., 1st sess.*, pp. 161, 183, 244, 292-293, 299-300, 324, 352-353.

[150] Especially, Calhoun and Butler, of South Carolina, Yulee, of Florida, Hunter and Mason, of Virginia, in the Senate, and Holmes, of South Carolina, and Meade, of Virginia, in the House. See for instance, *ibid.*, pp. 96, 185-186, 296, 310-311.

[151] For example, Niles, of Connecticut, *ibid.*, pp. 328-329.

[152] Butler, however, asserted that "Mexico has a right to complain of the exacting terms which we have been demanding of her as a price of peace." *Ibid.*, p. 186.

[153] *Ibid.*, pp. 96-97, 185-186, 310-311.

party and Calhoun Democrats which faced the expansionists.

A search for the members of Congress who were definitely in favor of the absorption of Mexico presents more difficulties. It may safely be asserted that most of the Democrats in both houses would offer no insuperable objections to annexation if there seemed to be no other practicable means of escape from the Mexican War; but more particularly identified with the expansionist movement were some twenty senators and representatives. Of these, there were none from New England, two from New York, three from the Southeast, and fifteen from the West and Southwest.[154] The attitude of members of Congress very naturally corresponded rather closely to public opinion in their constituencies. The expansionists seemed to be weakest in New England and strongest in New York and the West. Being a Whig stronghold, extremely hostile to slavery, and somewhat jealous of the increasing importance of the West, New England did not look with favor on the absorption of Mexico. The Southeast was divided between Whigs and Democrats, with all of the Whigs and some of the Democrats convinced that the absorption of Mexico would be dangerous to the peace and safety of the slavocracy and the Union. Accordingly opinion was divided with the opponents of extensive annexation being in a majority. Economic motives seem to have played an important rôle in converting the New Yorkers to the idea of the annexation of all Mexico. The West, aggressive, nationalistic, and predominently Democratic, needed little provocation to demand all the territory in sight.

An examination of the remarks made by most of the ex-

---

[154] From the Northeast, Senators Dickinson and Dix, of New York; from the Southeast, Senator Westcott, of Florida, and Representatives McLane, of Maryland, and Sims, of South Carolina; from the Southwest, Senators Lewis, of Alabama, Foote and Davis, of Mississippi, Houston and Rusk, of Texas, Sevier, of Arkansas, Turney, of Tennessee, Atchison, of Missouri, and Representatives Morse, of Louisiana, and Stanton, of Tennessee; from the Northwest, Senators Allen, of Ohio, Hannegan, of Indiana, Breese and Douglas, of Illinois, and Cass, of Michigan. *Cong. Globe, 30th Cong., 1st sess.*, January and February 1848; proceedings of the executive session of the Senate in connection with the ratification of the Treaty of Guadalupe Hidalgo, *30th Cong., 1st sess., S. Ex. Doc. No. 52*, pp. 1-37.

pansionists reveals practically everything but simplicity and directness. In many—perhaps most cases—speeches were designedly ambiguous in order that speakers might be able to modify their positions as circumstances seemed to demand. Senators Foote, of Mississippi, and Rusk, of Texas, may be taken as typical representatives of the southwestern contingent in Congress. After a long discourse on the economic advantages of Mexico and the danger of foreign intrigues south of the Rio Grande, Foote declared: " I am satisfied, Sir, for the present with having presented this hypothetical view of the compensating advantages likely to arise from the annexation of Mexico, in case the obstinacy of that nation . . . should finally constrain us to take possession of all the country." [155] When it was later intimated by a Whig that Foote was in favor of securing all Mexico, the Mississippian issued a vigorous denial: " He was opposed to such an idea, and he had gone as far as anyone. But if that country should be forced on us, we must endure all the good we can from it." [156] And who could blame the senator from Mississippi for that statement? Rusk informed the Senate that if there were any assurance that Mexico would not fall into the hands of a European power he would be satisfied with only a " small portion of her territory, by way of indemnity; but in the absence of all such security, he could not understand how the taking possession of all the territory, and guaranteeing the protection of the people, could be called robbery." [157] An unfriendly critic would say that Foote and Rusk were merely invoking Mexican obstinacy and the danger of European intervention to prepare the way for the absorption of Mexico, which would be entirely in accord with their desires.

Cass and Hannegan, representing northwestern Democrats, also exhibited the uncertainty common to the proponents of extensive annexations. Resolutions presented by

---

[155] *Cong. Globe, 30th Cong., 1st sess.*, pp. 219-221.

[156] *Ibid.*, p. 362.

[157] *Ibid.*, p. 375. For the attitude taken by Morse, Jefferson Davis and Sevier, see *ibid.*, pp. 280, 299, 302-303, 321. An interesting speech by Houston, delivered in New York, may be found in the New York *Herald*, 30 January 1848.

Hannegan stated that the United States would never submit to a monarchical government established in Mexico by the intervention of a foreign power. Furthermore, according to the senator from Indiana, it might " become necessary and proper, as it is within the constitutional capacity of this Government, for the United States to hold Mexico as a territorial appendage." [158] Cass assured the Senate, and incidentally the public, that if the United States " should swallow Mexico to-morrow " he did not believe " it would kill us." If the war should continue much longer the senator from Michigan thought that " we may have to make the great experiment so dreaded by the Senator from South Carolina and the Senator from Kentucky, and annex the dominions of Mexico to our own." [159] If it did become necessary to make the " dreaded experiment " of annexing Mexico, Cass and Hannegan, with all the West behind them, could be trusted to meet the danger without fear and trembling. But of course no one would ever think of such a thing unless driven to it by stark necessity.

On January 12, Senator Dickinson delivered an oration on the subject of the territorial destiny of the United States in general and the implications of the Mexican War in particular, which scarcely concealed his desire for all Mexico. The New Yorker contended that Mexico was more endangered by her own " imbecility and stubbornness " than by the war and its consequences. He pointed out, however, that Mexican mines, agricultural lands and Pacific harbors presented a great temptation to " European rapacity." Should the American army be withdrawn, " we may expect to see some supernumerary of the House of Bourbon placed at their head to play automaton to the British Cabinet." While

---

[158] *Cong. Globe, 30th Cong., 1st sess.*, p. 136.

[159] *Ibid.*, pp. 184, 216. These statements caused Cass considerable difficulty. They apparently conveyed more definite information than he intended to make public. On February 15, Upham, of Vermont, read some of Cass's remarks to the Senate as evidence of the existence of a demand for all Mexico. In reply, Cass stated that " he would now, for the third or fourth time, say, that he was entirely opposed to the annexation of all Mexico." *Ibid.*, p. 362.

Dickinson intimated that all Mexico would be annexed to the United States in time, he expressed his willingness to accept California and New Mexico for the time being. " We cannot virtuously continue the war," said he, " for the mere purpose of making further conquests; but we can virtuously continue it to the subjection of the whole of Mexico, if she will not make peace with us on just and honorable terms." [160] It is evident that if Mexico ever did agree to make peace on " just and honorable terms," Dickinson, for one, would be sadly disappointed. It is possible that the mines, lands and harbors of Mexico offered a temptation to American as well as foreign " rapacity."

Two days before Dickinson's harangue, Stanton, of Tennessee, delivered a speech in the House which for its simplicity and candor deserves mention. Stanton agreed with Calhoun " that the tendency of things was to the subjugation of the whole of Mexico. He believed it to be unavoidable, and he thought it desirable. At all events, come it would sooner or later." The President had asked for additional forces to serve in Mexico and Stanton hoped the House would grant them. They would not be used to conquer Mexico if she would agree to " proper terms of peace."

But he confessed he had no idea that they would have a Government willing to do this; and, unless they did it, and that shortly, neither they nor we could prevent the accomplishment of what he believed to be the great design of Providence in this whole movement. He apprehended none of those dangers which some gentlemen saw to our own liberties. He, for one, was in favor of pushing on the war, and giving the President every dollar he asked for. He did not fear such difficulties as some foresaw in carrying out the war to its results.[161]

There was no doubt about Stanton's attitude; he wanted all Mexico and made no secret of the fact that he thought the Mexican republic was doomed.

The remarks of Senator Sevier are of particular interest.

[160] *Ibid.*, pp. 157-158. On January 26, Senator Dix expressed sentiments similar to those of his colleague. *Ibid.*, pp. 250, 254-257.
[161] *Ibid.*, p. 135. Senator Breese, of Illinois, and Representative McLane, of Maryland, were no less frank in their statements. *Ibid.*, pp. 201, 350-351.

As Chairman of the Committee on Foreign Relations, Sevier was considered to be the spokesman in the Senate for the administration. On February 4, he refused to deny or affirm that California and New Mexico would be sufficient indemnity for the United States. The senator from Arkansas was in favor of advancing rather than retreating. By comparing the Mexicans with the Indians in the United States, Sevier undertook to prove that there would be no greater difficulty in "civilizing and governing the mass of the Mexicans" than had been encountered in dealing with the Indians. The United States would assume the debt of Mexico, but the increase in poulation would lighten the burden of payment.[162] The whole speech was hypothetical but to the Senate it meant that the President was beginning to catch up with the more extreme expansionists. That of course gave added strength to the sentiment for absorption. Just about forty-eight hours before this speech, however, in distant Mexico, Nicholas P. Trist and the Mexican representatives affixed their signatures to the Treaty of Guadalupe Hidalgo. It was now a question as to whether or not the expansionist movement had enough strength to destroy the work of the discredited Trist.

It would seem that time only was necessary to produce a very formidable sentiment for the acquisition of Mexico in the Congress. The movement for absorption was still in a more or less tentative stage at the middle of February, 1848, and was confined exclusively to Democrats. It is probable that Representative Stanton expressed in words what most western Democrats and many eastern Democrats thought but for one reason or another did not see fit to make public. Not many Democrats openly advocated the absorption of Mexico; but there were some who did and the number was increasing. Had the struggle with Mexico lasted much longer, perhaps all the Democrats except the Calhoun faction and a few New Englanders would have gradually become reconciled to the prospect of the absorption of Mexico.[163] Most of the support

---

[162] *Ibid.*, pp. 302-303.

[163] Late in January Senator Niles wrote to Van Buren that the designs of the administration and the partisans of Cass were becom-

for absorption was ostensibly based on the contention that Mexico would never sign a satisfactory treaty. As often as not, however, this was more in the nature of an excuse rather than a real reason. Those expansionists who pled necessity generally brought in such subjects as the destiny of the United States, the economic assets of Mexico, and the probability of European intrigues as additional reasons why Mexico should not be left to her own devices. In short, they were trying to construct the best case possible for absorption without offering an affront to Anglo-Saxon idealism by proposing sheer conquest as sufficient justification for taking Mexico. If public opinion should become so unmistakably in favor of absorption that there was no danger of misinterpreting the omens, increasing numbers of politicians would doubtless be able to express their sentiments in a more definite form.

And it did appear that the politicians might not have long to wait. There seemed to be no end to the Mexican War. The feeling that the absorption of Mexico was inevitable was gradually spreading throughout the United States—among the people, in the administration, and in Congress. The approaching presidential election made it necessary that the issue be faced. Accordingly in January and February, aspi-

ing more apparent. " Their object is the conquest of Mexico and its annexation to the United States. Cass to-day declared that the war was to be prosecuted for the conquest of Mexico, which he repeated several times. He afterwards explained that he was not for annexing or absorbing *all* of Mexico. This last step it only remains for him to [take], and as he has stepped one way fast, it will not be long before the last step will be taken. But his most . . . [ardent?] friends have taken the last step, and openly advocate the absorption of all Mexico. Of this number Dickinson takes the lead. Foot [sic] who is now speaking is another & the scope of his speech, is to that effect, so far as it tends to any practical result. Hannegan is another, & even Bagby is supposed to favor the scheme, and probably all our side except Mr. Calhoun and his friends (and how many there are of them I know not), and Gen Dix & myself will undoubtedly fall in with this scheme and go along with the current. . . ." Niles to Van Buren, 20 January 1848, Van Buren MSS. Niles was a follower of Van Buren and not a partisan of either Cass or the administration. He cannot, therefore, be depended upon to give an unbiased opinion of their objects. But in this case all the evidence seems to indicate that he was not far from the truth. By his own confession Niles was about to succumb to the fever himself.

rants for that high office and their friends were making desperate efforts to interpret and at the same time to direct the trend of public opinion.   Many of the Democrats, some of the Whigs and a few abolitionists had already joined, with varying degrees of frankness, the drive for all Mexico.   On the other hand, a majority of the Whig party and a group of slaveholding Democrats, for various reasons relating to politics and slavery, opposed the placing of the American flag in a permanent position over the " Halls of the Montezumas."   That was the situation when on February 19, the Treaty of Guadalupe Hidalgo was placed in the hands of the President of the United States.   Had Mexico agreed to terms of peace which the President and Senate would consider " just and honorable "?   If so the case of the expansionists had lost its principal justification and would probably collapse   The ensuing three weeks would furnish the answer to that question.

CHAPTER IV

DISAPPEARANCE

The demise of the sentiment for all Mexico occurred to all intents and purposes in the period from February 19 to March 10, 1848. It was the acceptance of the Treaty of Guadalupe Hidalgo by the United States which administered the death blow to the schemes of the expansionists. Of course there was a chance that Mexico would finally reject the treaty, and had that happened the annexationists might have carried the day sooner or later. But the treaty was not rejected by Mexico and as it actually happened the movement for absorption ceased to be a force in the United States after March, 1848. The story of the negotiations leading to the treaty which ended the war has been well and frequently told.[1] The famous quarrel between Commissioner Trist and General Winfield Scott, their equally famous reconciliation and subsequent friendship, furnish a most interesting and unique chapter in American diplomatic history, but as such are of no particular importance in connection with this study. The possibility of the absorption of Mexico, however, was one of the chief factors which induced Trist to ignore his recall and continue negotiations. The treaty which resulted from these negotiations was of the utmost importance in preventing the absorption of Mexico. Hence the story of the Treaty of Guadalupe Hidalgo in its relations to the expansionist movement records the death of that movement.

The full significance of the negotiation of the treaty cannot be understood without a knowledge of conditions in Mexico after the capture of Mexico City on September 14, 1847. Two days after that event Santa Anna resigned the Presidency which then fell into the hands of Peña y Peña,

---

[1] Jesse S. Reeves, " The Treaty of Guadalupe Hidalgo," *American Historical Review*, X, 309-324; Rives, *The United States and Mexico, 1821-1848*, II, 423-432, 440-447, 500-522, 584-613; Smith, *The War with Mexico*, II, 127-139, 233-240; McCormac, *James K. Polk*, pp. 487-537; Louis M. Sears, " Nicholas P. Trist, a Diplomat with Ideals," *Mississippi Valley Historical Review*, XI, 85-98.

one of the leaders of the *moderado* party. The *moderados* were desirous of peace, opposed to all dictators of Santa Anna's type, and supporters of existing institutions in Mexico. Scarcely less numerous than the *moderados* were the *puros*, a radical republican party which did not desire peace until the old Mexican army should have been virtually exterminated. A large number of *puros* favored annexation to the United States as the best safeguard for order and prosperity. The Santanistas and the monarchists were also opposed to peace but for entirely different reasons from those advanced by the *puros*. The supporters of Santa Anna hoped that their leader would be restored to power and thus be able to bestow favors on his adherents. " Santa Anna's talents could be exercised only in troubled times, so that a program like Guizot's, offering only peace and bourgeois prosperity, promised nothing for faithful followers." [2] The monarchists were opposed to peace because they were opposed to anything which seemed likely to strengthen the forces making for republicanism in Mexico. The *moderados*, however, held the reins of government for the time being, albeit on a rather precarious tenure of doubtful legality. President Peña and his party were determined to have peace if possible, but quick action was necessary as the government might at any time succumb to its foes. It seemed that now or never peace would be made.[3]

Commissioner Trist, doubtless realizing the possibilities of the situation, undertook, on October 20, to reopen negotiations.[4] On October 21, the Mexican foreign minister notified Trist that although there seemed to be little hope for an agreement commissioners would be appointed in a "few days" to continue the negotiations.[5] This was the state of affairs when the American commissioner received notice of

[2] Rives, II, 59.
[3] *Ibid.*, pp. 568, 590-592; Smith, II, 233-236; Trist to Buchanan, 25 October 1847, Trist MSS; Parrott to Marcy, 20 December 1847, Marcy MSS.
[4] Trist to Luis de la Rosa, 20 October 1847, Trist MSS.
[5] Luis de la Rosa to Trist, 31 October 1847, *ibid.*

his recall on November 16. Poor communications between Vera Cruz and Mexico City resulted in Buchanan's dispatch of October 6, and a later one dated October 25, being placed in Trist's hands at the same time. When the latter dispatch was written the Washington government had official information concerning the negotiations which had broken down early in September. Trist was severely reprimanded for offering to refer the Nueces-Rio Grande question to Washington and was again directed to leave Mexico.[6] The peace negotiations seemed destined to end in failure again. Given the conditions in Mexico the results might be disastrous in their effect on the peace party. The *moderado* government could scarcely survive the loss of prestige which would be occasioned by the collapse of its peace program. The fall of the *moderados* might mean the end of independent Mexico.

Until December 4, Trist fully intended to obey his instructions and leave Mexico at the first suitable opportunity. On this date, however, he suddenly decided to remain and continue his efforts to secure a treaty on the basis of the *sine qua non* provided in his instructions of April, 1847;[7] that is, the Rio Grande boundary for Texas and the cession of Upper California and New Mexico to the United States for a money payment. To make a long story short, after much procrastination on the part of the Mexicans, the Treaty of Guadalupe Hidalgo was signed on February 2, and forwarded to Washington.[8] Under the terms of the treaty Mexico surrendered Upper California and New Mexico and gave up all claims to the territory between the Nueces and the Rio Grande. In return the United States agreed to pay fifteen million dollars and assume all unpaid claims of its citizens

---

[6] Buchanan to Trist, 25 October 1847, *ibid.* Along with this dispatch went a letter from Buchanan expressing regret at the necessity of having to write such a communication, but pointing out that it was unavoidable under the circumstances. *Ibid.*

[7] Trist to Mrs. Trist, 4 December 1847, and Trist to Thornton, 4 December 1847, *ibid.*

[8] For details, see Rives, II, 598-613; Smith, II, 238-241; McCormac, pp. 536-538.

against Mexico.[9] Mexico had finally agreed to give up the minimum amount of territory which had been demanded of her nine months before as the price of peace. She received, however, five million dollars less than Trist had been authorized to pay in the preceding April. The problem now was: would such a treaty be acceptable to the President and Senate of the United States? Before discussing the fate of the treaty in the United States we may turn our attention to the part played by the threatened absorption of Mexico in causing Trist to continue negotiations.

The belief that Mexico would be annexed by the United States if he left that country without a treaty, seems to have had considerable weight in determining Trist's conduct after his recall.[10] The commissioner's correspondence shows that he reasoned somewhat as follows: the *puros* were anxious to secure a permanent connection with the United States and would do everything in their power to prevent the closing of the war;[11] a breakdown in negotiations would strengthen the *puros* and weaken the *moderados,* whose prestige and continuance in power depended on the negotiation of a peace;[12] the cession of New Mexico and Upper California was the greatest concession that the Mexican government could make;[13] if the present opportunity were not seized at once all chance of making a treaty would be lost, perhaps for all

---

[9] A copy of the treaty may be found in *30th Cong., 1st sess., S. Ex. Doc. No. 52,* pp. 38-66; William M. Malloy, comp., *Treaties, Conventions, International Acts, Protocols and Agreements between the United States of America and Other Powers,* I, 681-692.

[10] The American commissioner received plenty of aid from General Scott in arriving at his decisions. Edward Thornton, an attaché of the British legation at Mexico, who had been an intermediary in the negotiations between Trist and the Mexicans also offered his advice. With British interests in view. no doubt, Thornton intimated to Trist that Mexico's existence as a nation was threatened if a treaty were not immediately secured. Winfield Scott, *Autobiography,* p. 576; Thornton to Trist, 22 November 1847, Trist MSS; McCormac, pp. 520, 522; Sears, pp. 94-96.

[11] Trist to Buchanan, 25 October, 29 December 1847, Trist MSS.

[12] Trist to Buchanan, 27 November 1847, Trist to Thornton, 4 December 1847, *ibid.*

[13] Trist to Thornton, 4 December 1847, Trist to Buchanan, 6 December 1847, *ibid.*

time;[14] the President of the United States was apparently determined to annex all Mexico;[15] ultimate absorption might be desirable, but a dissolution of the Union would be better than immediate annexation.[16] In other words, Trist thought that conditions in both Mexico and the United States pointed to an indefinite continuance of a state of war, with the absorption of Mexico as a probable result, if he obeyed his instructions. This consummation of events he desired to prevent. Hence his determination to negotiate a treaty if possible.

Whether Trist really desired to further the interests of his country as he saw them or whether he was interested in embarrassing the President is a moot question,[17] and is not germane to this discussion. In any event the result was the same. The significant fact is that with the exception of his estimate as to Polk's intentions Trist, with Scott's and Thornton's help, had correctly interpreted the trend of events. It seems certain that had they not been faced with a *fait accompli* the Washington authorities would have demanded more territory from Mexico than was secured by the Treaty of Guadalupe Hidalgo. It is likewise probable that no Mexi-

---

[14] *Ibid.*

[15] The notice of his recall and intimations from Buchanan that the administration and the people were no longer satisfied with the terms previously offered Mexico seem to have convinced Trist that Polk had designs on all Mexico. In a long dispatch, dated December 6, the commissioner explained his reasons for ignoring his recall. The whole dispatch indicated that Trist thought that the President desired to annex Mexico. Buchanan to Trist, 6 , 7, 24, October 1847, Trist MSS; Trist to Buchanan, 6 December 1847, *ibid.*; Reeves, p. 322.

[16] Trist to Buchanan, 6 December 1847, Trist MSS.

[17] At this time Trist was General Scott's boon companion. The General was very bitter toward the Washington authorities and Trist, himself, resented the attitude of the administration concerning his conduct of the negotiations before his recall. Scott was engaged in a controversy with General Pillow, who was Polk's intimate friend, and Trist entered the lists with great vigor against Pillow whom he considered as the mouthpiece of the President. It is likely that Trist was not entirely free from feelings of malice toward Polk when he undertook, with Scott's approval, to rescue his country from the dangers which threatened her. On this subject, see Smith, II, 237-238; Sears, pp. 94-98; Reeves, pp. 321-322; McCormac, pp. 520, 525-526.

can government could or would have taken the initiative in proposing the cession of New Mexico and California. Much less were the chances that the Mexicans would have ever agreed to the cession of additional territories. At best much time would have elapsed before such an agreement could have been reached. In the meantime the sentiment for the absorption of Mexico in the United States would have had time to develop its full strength. It seems, therefore, that Trist took the only step which under the circumstances could have prevented the absorption of Mexico.

Meanwhile, before the news that Trist would refuse to obey his orders had reached Washington, Polk had become convinced that the power to treat with Mexico should be conferred on someone. On December 31, Senators Cass and Jefferson Davis called on the President. Davis read to Polk a communication from General Twiggs to the effect that if a commissioner with diplomatic powers were in Mexico a treaty might be concluded. Both senators advised that such an agent be appointed. Senator Davis thought that if Mexico were forced to send negotiators to the United States the government which appointed them would probably be overthrown before they could return to Mexico and they would as likely as not be treated as traitors when they did get back home.[18] This advice was good and it seems to have appealed to Polk, for the subject was immediately taken up in the cabinet. Differences of opinion as to who should be appointed prevented any definite action on the matter.[19] This apparent willingness to give Mexico another chance to accept peace proposals coming from the United States would probably have accomplished little as Polk had determined to demand more territory than Upper California and New Mexico.[20]

---

[18] Polk's *Diary*, III, 269-270. Cass and Davis were shortly afterwards to take the position that the Sierra Madre Mountains would be a proper boundary for the United States. *Cong. Globe, 30th Cong., 1st sess.*, pp. 293, 299. One wonders if their advice to Polk was sincerely given or whether they were trying to accomplish by indirection the absorption of Mexico. If Mexico would accept the Sierra Madre line, well and good, but did Cass and Davis think that she would ever agree to meet such terms?

[19] Polk's *Diary*, III, 275-276, 280.   [20] *Ibid.*, pp. 276-277.

On January 4, all plans for appointing another negotiator were dropped for information was received at Washington which indicated that the United States already had a representative in Mexico who would treat for peace whether he had the power to do so or not.[21] The next day Buchanan informed the President that he had seen a letter from Trist to his wife which stated that a treaty would be made if the Mexicans would agree to the ultimatum laid down in the instructions of April, 1847.[22] Finally on the fifteenth, a long, garrulous and insulting dispatch from Trist, announcing his plans and giving reasons for not leaving Mexico, was placed in the hands of the President.[23] Polk was greatly incensed at the conduct of Trist. He concluded that the commissioner had become the " menial instrument " of General Scott in a dark conspiracy against the administration.[24] The President immediately told Secretary Marcy to send a dispatch to General Butler [25] directing him to order Trist away from army headquarters and to notify the authorities of Mexico that the commissioner no longer had any authority to represent the United States.[26]

The sending of Marcy's dispatch was delayed several days while the question of what was to be done in case Trist had already signed a treaty was being considered. To send such notice to the Mexican government might embarrass the President unless he had determined to reject any treaty made by Trist. On January 23, Sevier and Cass advised Polk to notify Mexico that Trist had been recalled. Sevier, however, thought that if a treaty had been completed the President would be bound to submit it to the Senate, while Cass, listening intently to the voice of the people, suggested that it might be better to wait until the treaty should be received

[21] *Ibid.*, pp. 282-283.
[22] *Ibid.*, p. 286.
[23] Trist to Buchanan, 6 December 1847, Trist MSS.
[24] Polk's *Diary*, III, 286, 300-301.
[25] Butler had succeeded Scott as commander of the army in Mexico.
[26] Polk's *Diary*, III, 301.

before making any decision. Both senators agreed that they
did not now approve of the terms of a treaty made in accord-
ance with Trist's ultimatum.[27] For the next three days the
problem was discussed by the President and members of the
cabinet. Marcy and Mason thought a treaty made in con-
formance with the terms formerly authorized should be submitted to the Senate. Walker and Buchanan felt that such
a treaty ought to be rejected. Buchanan, however, " saw
embarrassments attending that course, and said he would not
now commit himself on the subject." Polk was inclined to
refuse to accept the treaty but since he, too, was aware of
" embarrassments " the President expressed doubts as to the
proper course to pursue. In spite of this doubt it was finally
decided to send notice of the revocation of Trist's diplomatic
powers to the Mexican government.[28]

The dispatch prepared by Secretary Marcy directed General
Butler to inform the Mexican authorities that Trist " would
be no longer recognized . . . as authorized to continue the
negotiation." If the Mexicans had any propositions to submit
they would be forwarded to Washington by the commanding
general. Butler was also ordered to notify Trist that he
should " no longer regard himself as being at the headquarters of the army, under the orders of his government."
If on the other hand a treaty had actually been signed, no
statement was to be made to the authorities of Mexico as in
that case Washington would attend to the matter.[29] In short,
the President had not decided to refuse to accept his former
ultimatum as a " just and honorable peace." Nevertheless, if
Trist had not already made a treaty Polk did not intend to
give him an opportunity to complete the task.

There were several reasons why the President found himself

---

[27] *Ibid.*, p. 310. Senator Hannegan also thought it would be
" very embarrassing " for Polk to reject a treaty made on the basis
of Trist's instruction; but neither did he now approve of such a
treaty. *Ibid.*, p. 315. Apparently Trist might be able to place an
obstacle in the path of the expansionists.

[28] *Ibid.*, pp. 310, 311, 314-317.

[29] Marcy to Butler, 26 January 1848, Marcy MSS; *30th Cong.,
1st sess., S. Ex. Doc. No. 52*, pp. 146-147.

in an embarrassing situation. He was thoroughly disgusted with Trist and naturally was not anxious to accept any treaty which might be made by his erstwhile negotiator, though the mere fact that Trist was acting without authority probably caused him little disquietude.[30] The cession of Upper California and New Mexico no longer satisfied Polk's territorial aspirations; but to refuse a treaty which secured those territories might seem inconsistent in view of Trist's instructions and numerous orations on the subject of a " just and honorable peace." Then, too, the Whigs had control of the purse strings of the republic and it could not be foreseen just what they might do if the President should give them the slightest justification for withholding supplies for the war. These are doubtless some of the thoughts which passed through Polk's mind as he anxiously awaited news from Mexico.

On February 19, the uncertainty existing at Washington was relieved by the arrival, after night, of the Treaty of Guadalupe Hidalgo. The treaty provided that the United States should receive New Mexico and Upper California, the boundary line to extend up the Rio Grande River to the southern boundary of New Mexico, thence along that boundary to its western termination, thence northward to the first branch of the Gila River, thence along the branch and the main stream of the Gila to the Rio Colorado, thence along the line between Upper and Lower California to the Pacific.[31] As soon as he knew the contents of the treaty Polk wrote in his diary:

> Mr. Trist was recalled in October last, but chose to remain in Mexico and continue the negotiations. The terms of the Treaty are within his instructions which he took out in April last, upon the important question of boundary and limits. There are many provisions in it which will require more careful examination than a single reading will afford. Mr. Trist has acted very badly, as I have heretofore noted in this diary, but notwithstanding this, if on further examination the Treaty is one that can be accepted, it should not be rejected on account of his bad conduct.[32]

---

[30] McCormac, p. 538.
[31] *30th Cong., 1st sess., S. Ex. Doc. No. 52*, p. 43; Malloy, I, 1109-1110.
[32] Polk's *Diary*, III, 345; McCormac, p. 538.

The tone of this entry indicates that the President had apparently made up his mind before the treaty arrived to accept an agreement made in conformity with Trist's instructions.

Since he had doubtless already decided that the treaty should be submitted to the Senate, Polk was very anxious to settle the business as soon as possible. So anxious was he that the question was referred to the cabinet on the day after the arrival of the treaty, even though in so doing the President violated his custom of not attending to business on Sunday. Walker and Buchanan advised that the treaty be rejected while Mason, Marcy, Johnson and Clifford suggested that it be submitted to the Senate. All the cabinet agreed that Article X which dealt with land grants in the ceded territories should be stricken out. Walker, of course, had long been in favor of the absorption of Mexico and his attitude caused no comment. The President, however, seems to have been irritated at the course of Buchanan. The Secretary of State insisted that the Sierra Madre Mountains should be made the boundary between the United States and Mexico. When Polk charged Buchanan with inconsistency, the Secretary replied that he had opposed the advance on Mexico City but had been overruled; that since the preceding April much blood and treasure had been spent; and that, consequently, he was not now satisfied with the treaty.[33] Buchanan neglected to mention the fact that his attitude was determined primarily with reference to the presidential campaign which was then under

___

[33] Polk's *Diary*, III, 346-351. As a matter of fact, Polk had known for over a month that Buchanan favored securing all territory east of the Sierra Madre range. At that time the President, himself, had expressed his intention of acquiring, in addition to Upper California and New Mexico, Lower California, the right of transit across the Isthmus of Tehuantepec and Tampico. *Ibid.*, pp. 276-277. Since the first of January, then, Buchanan had been more consistent than his chief. But Polk had conceived the idea that the Secretary of State did not wish to incur the disfavor of those who desired the conquest of all Mexico. In the President's opinion, Buchanan wanted him to submit the treaty to the Senate against the advice of the Secretary of State. If the treaty were approved, Buchanan would gain prestige as a member of the administration; if it were rejected the Secretary could call the attention of the public to his opposition. *Ibid.*, p. 350. Polk may not have been correct in this assump-

way. No definite conclusion as to what to do with the treaty was reached at this time.[34]

On February 21, Polk informed the cabinet that he had decided to accept the document. As was usually the case, the President very carefully recorded the reasons for his decision. The treaty conformed on the main question of limits to the instructions given to Trist in April, 1847; although more territory, perhaps the Sierra Madre line, would be demanded if a treaty were still to be made, it was not likely that this could ever be secured with the consent of Mexico; if Trist's treaty were rejected, even the territories acquired under its provisions might be lost since the Whig opposition in the House could force a gradual withdrawal of the army from Mexico; should the Whigs elect the next President it was probable that the country would lose all the advantages secured by the treaty; if the Chief Executive should reject his own terms offered to Mexico in the preceding April, he did not see how it was possible for his administration to be sustained.[35] On the next day, Polk sent the treaty to the Senate giving it favorable recommendations with the exception of the tenth article and a secret article concerning the time of ratification.[36]

Truly, the Treaty of Guadalupe Hidalgo seriously hindered the President's plans of expansion as they were maturing in January and February, 1848. Starting at the beginning of the war with a determination to secure Upper California and New Mexico in any event, Polk had decided by January, 1848, to also acquire Lower California and Tampico. Indeed, there

tion, but there is no doubt that political considerations played an important rôle in the career of James Buchanan.

[34] *Ibid.*, pp. 346-347. For an account of the cabinet session of February 20, prepared by Polk's private secretary, see Polk MSS.

[35] Polk's *Diary*, III, 347-348; McCormac, p. 540; Bourne, *American Historical Review*, V, 500. It seems that Walker and Buchanan talked of resigning on account of the controversy over the treaty. Polk's *Diary*, III, 359. But since their opposition was known as early as February 23, the two Secretaries probably felt that they would gain nothing by resigning. Washington correspondent of the New Orleans *Picayune*, 3 March 1848.

[36] Polk's *Diary*, III, pp. 351, 352. For the message to Congress, see *30th Cong., 1st sess., S. Ex. Doc. No. 52*, pp. 3-4.

are indications that he was preparing to demand a boundary formed by the Sierra Madre Mountains. The President seems to have realized that he might have trouble in getting Mexico to agree to surrender such large portions of her territory. In that case he was prepared to recommend a continued occupation of Mexico until " full indemnity " should be secured. This continued occupation might, and probably would, have become a permanent affair.

But in April, 1847, Nicholas P. Trist had been sent to Mexico, carrying the project of a treaty which provided for the cession of Upper California and New Mexico and the acknowledgement of the Rio Grande as the boundary of Texas. Trist at first failed to secure a treaty. He was recalled but did not see fit to obey orders from Washington. When the President found out that his negotiator might be able to secure New Mexico and Upper California, he did everything possible to prevent the completion of a treaty along those lines. This was undoubtedly due in part to Polk's disgust with Trist; but it was also due to some extent to the fact that the President wanted more territory. When in spite of all executive efforts Mexico did agree to cede Upper California and New Mexico, Polk was forced to accept the cession, not because he was satisfied but because he felt that under the circumstances there was nothing else to do.[37] It may be said at once that the President apparently did not desire all Mexico, but it does seem that he was prevented from pursuing a policy which tended in that direction by the conduct of Commissioner Trist. If the embarrassment of the President or the prevention of the absorption of Mexico, or both, were the ends which Trist hoped to achieve, he had certainly accomplished the former, and had gone far toward success in the latter, when the Treaty of Guadalupe Hidalgo was submitted to the Senate.

For sometime before the arrival of the treaty rumors concerning a peace treaty had been appearing in the press.[38]

---

[37] On the subject of Polk's motives, see McCormac, p. 541; Smith, II, 244-246; Rippy, *The United States and Mexico*, p. 19.
[38] New York *Herald*, 1 February 1848; *Democratic Review*, XXII, 279.

Three days after the document had been received at Washington the New York *Herald* published the terms of a proposed treaty which Trist had submitted to the Mexicans on August 27, 1847. The editor asserted that the document just received contained similar provisions and this seems to have gained general credence.[39] Such papers as the Charleston *Mercury*, the Boston *Post* and the *National Era* advocated ratification on the grounds that the treaty was a good one and here was a chance to stop the effusion of blood and end an interminable war which might lead to the absorption of Mexico.[40] The *New Englander*, together with outspoken expansionist organs like the New York *Herald*, the *Democratic Review* and the New Orleans *Mercury* took the view that no treaty with Mexico was worth the paper on which it was written, and hence by implication advised its rejection.[41] The Whig Boston *Atlas* considered that the irregular status of Trist was sufficient reason for condemning his handiwork.[42] But the editor of the national organ [43] of the Whig party refused to prepare an article against ratification, while the New York *Tribune*, also Whig, frankly called for Whig support for the treaty since an " endless foreign war " was " worse than any honorable treaty of peace could be." [44]

If the papers here mentioned may be considered as typical representatives of the press there was not a great amount of enthusiasm for the treaty of peace. Yet for various reasons it would receive support from Whig as well as Democratic sources. It is fairly certain that some journals like the Whig New York *Tribune* and the Democratic Charleston *Mercury* were afraid that if the treaty were rejected the absorption of all Mexico would follow. The Boston *Post*, in fact, warned

---

[39] New York *Herald*, 22 February 1848.
[40] Charleston *Mercury*, 25 February 1848; *National Era*, 24 February 1848; Boston *Post*, 6 March 1848.
[41] *New Englander*, VI, 292; New York *Herald*, 25, 26 February 1848; *Democratic Review*, XXII, 280; New Orleans *Mercury*, quoted by the Boston *Post*, 4 March 1848.
[42] Boston *Atlas*, quoted by the Boston *Post*, 9 March 1848.
[43] *National Intelligencer*. See McCormac, p. 547.
[44] New York *Tribune*, quoted by the Boston *Post*, 9 March 1848.

the Whigs that such would be the result if ratification failed.[45] The interesting thing to note is that even such an unqualified advocate of the annexation of Mexico as the New York *Herald* did not deem it expedient to oppose the treaty because it did not secure enough territory. No doubt the *Herald* along with many other journals was not satisfied with Upper California and New Mexico; but the movement for absorption had been, to a considerable extent, based on the alleged impossibility of forcing Mexico to agree to an honorable peace. There had not been sufficient time for the development of any great amount of sentiment for absorption on its own account. The expansionist press was thus reduced to the necessity of trying to show that the treaty did not provide for a real peace. It was an uphill fight and the adherents of the acquisition of all Mexico were soon to be defeated.

The death of John Quincy Adams on February 23, delayed for a few days the Senate's action on the treaty. By preventing the formation of hasty decisions and instilling a feeling of seriousness in the minds of senators, the passing of Adams probably tended to increase the chances of ratification.[46] In spite of that, however, reports were not encouraging. It was rumored that Buchanan and Walker were exerting their influence against the treaty.[47] The Washington correspondent of the New York *Courier* expected serious opposition from " Wilmot Proviso " senators of the North and Calhoun Democrats of the South.[48] " Galviensis " declared that some senators, among them Houston and Rusk, would vote against the treaty because they wanted more territory.[49] " Sierra Madre " was convinced that ten other western senators would join Houston and Rusk because they, too, were not satisfied with

---

[45] Boston *Post*, 6 March 1848.

[46] Smith, II, 246; Rives, II, 629-630.

[47] Polk's *Diary*, III, 361-362; " Sierra Madre " in the New York *Herald*, 25 February 1848.

[48] New York *Courier*, quoted by *Niles' Register*, LXXIII, 416. There never was any doubt, however, about the attitude of Calhoun. On February 23, the Carolinian wrote that ratification would be a " fortunate deliverance " for the country. *Correspondence of Calhoun*, p. 744.

[49] New York *Herald*, 24 February 1848.

the amount of territory acquired from Mexico.[50] One observer counted twenty-one Democrats who could be expected to oppose ratification, though the number was reduced when the writer became convinced that Calhoun, Butler, Yulee and Hunter would not vote with the opposition.[51] Another correspondent was sure that several senators were opposed to the treaty because they wanted to acquire all the Mexican territory. But, said he, " a very small portion, if any, advocate openly, the whole of Mexico." [52] Summing it all up, " Galviensis " concluded that while there were not six men in the Senate who approved of the treaty there would not be six men who would vote against it. This very astute correspondent reported that there was a " mistaken idea " among senators that the people wanted peace.[53] These were nothing but rumors but they indicate that competent observers on the spot expected as much opposition to a ratification from western expansionists as from any other group. It was also suspected that the opposition of some of the expansionists came from their desire to acquire all Mexico even though they did not make public admission of the fact.

Much more substantial as evidence of senatorial opposition to the treaty was the fact that the Committee on Foreign Relations had determined to recommend its rejection. On February 28, Chairman Sevier informed Polk that all the members of the committee except himself were in favor of sending a commission to Mexico to negotiate another treaty. The other members, Webster, Mangum, Hannegan and Benton did not object, said Sevier, to the provisions of the treaty, but they objected to its having been negotiated by an unauthorized agent. Sevier had called with the knowledge of the committee to get Polk's views on the subject. The President was decidedly opposed to the proposed plan.

---

[50] *Ibid.*, 25 February 1848.
[51] Letter dated February 25, Washington correspondent of the New Orleans *Picayune*, 4 March 1848.
[52] Washington correspondent of the New York *Courier*, quoted by *Niles' Register*, LXXIII, 416.
[53] New York *Herald*, 24 February 1848.

I told him I condemned the insubordinate & insolent conduct of Mr. Trist, but that the Treaty itself was the subject for consideration and not his conduct, and that if the provisions of the Treaty were such as could be accepted, it would be worse than an idle ceremony to send out such a commission to re-negotiate the same Treaty. . . . Mr. Sevier informed me that Mr. Webster said he wanted *no* territory beyond the Rio Grande. . . . I do not wonder at his course, but I am surprised at that of Mr. Hannegan and Mr. Benton. Extremes sometimes meet and act effectively for negative purposes but never for affirmative purposes. They have done so in this instance. Mr. Webster is for *no* territory and Mr. Hannegan is for *all* Mexico, and for opposite reasons both will oppose the Treaty. It is difficult upon any rational principle, to assign a satisfactory reason for anything Col. Benton may do, especially in his present temper of mind, wholly engrossed as he has been for some months past with the case of his son-in-law, Col. Fremont.[54]

Polk had undoubtedly unearthed the combination which was likely to defeat the treaty if it were defeated. Many of the Whigs, including Webster, had said so much about their opposition to the acquisition of territory that it would require considerable mental agility for them to vote for the Treaty of Guadalupe Hidalgo. It was a question whether many of them could perform the feat. On the other hand, many Democrats, including Hannegan, would be glad to see the United States extend as far as the Sierra Madre Mountains, the Isthmus of Tehuantepec or Cape Horn. If many in these two camps stuck to their guns the treaty was doomed. The first victory, however, went to the forces in favor of ratification when after hearing from the President the committee

---

[54] Polk's *Diary*, III, 363-366. It may be said that Benton contended that Texas extended no farther than the Nueces River and he had been lukewarm in his support of the war. *Ibid.*, I, 390; *Cong. Globe, 29th Cong., 1st sess.*, p. 798; Thomas H. Benton, *Thirty Years View*, II, 600-601. In addition the Missourian had become estranged from Polk on account of Fremont's conviction for insubordination. He had refused to serve as Chairman of the Committee on Military Affairs and in February, 1848, he was hardly on speaking terms with the President. Polk's *Diary*, III, 204, 228-229; Benton, II, 715-719; McCormac, pp. 475-477. In so far as a logical reason for Benton's attitude toward the treaty may be discovered, it would seem that he opposed it because too much territory was secured. The senator from Missouri, however, was predisposed to view with alarm any measure proposed by the Polk administration. Rives suggests that Benton opposed the treaty because the United States got too little territory, but there seems to be no evidence to support this theory. Rives, II, 636-637.

reported the treaty to the Senate without recommendation on the same day.[55]

For several days a battle royal raged in the Senate. Opposition came from non-expansionist Whigs and expansionist Democrats.[55a] For the Whigs, resolutions by Webster, Baldwin, of Connecticut, Badger, of North Carolina, and Crittenden, of Kentucky, introduced the subjects of Trist's lack of authority, slavery and too much territory into the discussion. These resolutions were either tabled or failed of passage. But analysis of the votes shows that all the Whigs except Johnson, of Maryland, Bell, of Tennessee, and Johnson, of Louisiana, would prefer to acquire no territory from Mexico.[56] Among the Democrats, Houston and Jefferson Davis offered resolutions: the one proposing that the United States take all territory as far south as Tampico; the other suggesting that the whole or a greater part of Coahuila, Chihuahua, Nuevo Leon and Tamaulipas should be acquired in addition to the territory ceded by the treaty.[57] Houstan's resolutions were never considered by the Senate, but it was disclosed that ten other Democratic senators from Florida, New York and the West, agreed with the Senator from Mississippi.[58] If the Whig exponents of " no territory " and the Democratic believers in " more territory " carried their opposition to the length of voting against the treaty, there was no chance for ratification.

[55] *30th Cong., 1st sess., S. Ex. Doc. No. 52*, p. 4. Polk was no doubt further encouraged when Walker and Buchanan told him " that they were utterly opposed to its [the treaty's] rejection & sending a fresh commission to Mexico to do the same thing. Mr. Walker was very excited, and thought the object of Mr. Webster was to defeat the acquisition of any territory. Mr. Buchanan and Mr. Walker left my office after night to visit Senators and urge them to vote against the project of [a] new commission to Mexico." Polk's *Diary*, III, 366. It may be that the Secretaries while they were engaged in the business of lobbying also urged the senators to vote against the treaty.

[55a] There is an excellent treatment of the proceedings in the Senate in Rives, II, 633-637.

[56] *30th Cong., 1st sess., S. Ex. Doc. No. 52*, pp. 4, 9, 22-23, 24-25, 32.

[57] *Ibid.*, pp. 5-6, 18.

[58] Those voting with Davis were Westcott, of Florida, Lewis, of Alabama, Houston and Rusk, of Texas, Turney, of Tennessee, Atchison, of Missouri, Douglas, of Illinois, Hannegan, of Indiana, Allen, of Ohio, and Dickinson, of New York. *Ibid.*, p. 18.

If on the other hand these resolutions and votes represented, for the most part, nothing but protests known to be futile and political maneuvers, then there was still hope.

And there were several reasons why many of those who did not favor the treaty would vote for it in spite of their disapproval. From the viewpoint of those who were opposed to expansion, delay in ending the war meant that all Mexico would probably be annexed.[59] This was a result much more to be deplored than the acquisition of Upper California and New Mexico alone. Many senators, therefore, might be expected to submit to the cession of Upper California and New Mexico in the belief that by so doing they were preventing the absorption of all Mexico. Then, too, those who are opposed to the Hamilton-Webster system of political economy, with its high tariff, saw in the continuance of the war an increasing likelihood of the enactment of such a tariff.[60] They could be expected to fall in line behind the treaty. Furthermore, the Whigs, who included in their ranks most of the protectionists and might, therefore, be supposed to desire to continue the war, were afraid that if the struggle kept on it would mean Whig defeat at the polls in November. There was hope, then, that many of those who would oppose the treaty on its own merits, would feel constrained to support ratification because of other considerations.

There is no record of the debates on the treaty, but Polk kept in touch with several senators and his diary contains interesting comments on the proceedings. On March 1, it was reported that ratification was doubtful. The Whigs had held a caucus and it was thought they would vote against the treaty.[61] On March 3, the President's information led him to believe that Webster and Benton were the leaders of the opposition. " Eight or ten, perhaps twelve Senators, it is

---

[59] This belief was very evident in most of the speeches made in Congress before the arrival of the treaty. *Cong. Globe, 30th Cong., 1st sess.,* January and February, 1848.

[60] On this subject, see Boucher, *In Re that Aggressive Slavocracy,* p. 35.

[61] Polk's *Diary,* III, 368-369; " W " in New York *Herald,* 4 March 1848.

said, will act with **Mr. Benton**; and six or eight Whig
Senators with Mr. Webster." The Democrats, in Polk's esti-
mation, were animated by a desire for more territory while
the Whigs wanted none at all.[62] Beginning Monday, March
6, reports were more favorable, and on the seventh, Polk
began to consider the appointment of a commissioner to take
the treaty to Mexico.[63] Finally, on March 10, the President
learned that by a vote of thirty-eight to fourteen, four senators
not voting, the Senate had given its consent to ratification
with amendments which did not affect the territorial provisions but which Polk thought might cause rejection by
Mexico.[64]

The vote in the Senate was neither partisan nor sectional.[65]
Twenty-six Democrats and twelve Whigs from all sections of
the country voted in the affirmative. The fourteen negative
votes were equally divided between Whigs and Democrats.
Five northern and two southern Whigs [66] joined one southern
and six western Democrats [67] in registering their opposition to
the treaty. One Democrat, Houston, of Texas, and three
Whigs, Phelps, of Vermonts, Clayton, of Delaware, and Pearce,
of Maryland, did not vote.[68] Had they all voted in the negative the treaty would still have been approved, though by a
very slender margin. As has already been indicated, many
votes were cast for the treaty without reference to its merits.
It might be added that public opinion seemed to be in favor
of peace.[69] Senators who wanted more or less territory than

---

[62] Polk's *Diary*, III, 370.   [63] *Ibid.*, pp. 372-373.   [64] *Ibid.*, p. 377.
[65] *30th Cong., 1st sess., S. Ex. Doc. No. 52*, p. 36; Rives, II, 636-
637.
[66] Baldwin, of Connecticut, Corwin, of Ohio, Spruance, of Delaware, Upham, of Vermont, Webster, of Massachusetts, Badger, of
North Carolina, and Berrien, of Georgia.
[67] Westcott, of Florida, Allen, of Ohio, Breese and Douglas, of
Illinois, Atchison and Benton, of Missouri, and Lewis, of Alabama.
[68] Houston would have probably voted against the treaty, but he
had been called to New Hampshire to deliver some addresses. Perhaps he concluded that this was the easiest method of escape. According to the Washington correspondent of the New Orleans *Picayune*, the Texan desired to convince the New Hampshire abolitionists
that he was " a gentleman and not a savage." New Orleans *Picayune*, 15 March 1848.
[69] Smith, II, 247; Rives, II, 630-631.

was provided by the treaty did not in many cases have the hardihood to put their votes on record against a treaty, the rejection of which meant a continuance of the war. It seems, however, that one important reason why most of the Whigs and Calhoun Democrats supported ratification was the fear that defeat for the treaty meant the complete realization of the expansionist program—the annexation of Mexico.[70] To the slaveholding Whigs and the Calhounites the annexation of Mexico would be pregnant with danger to the interests of slavery. The Whig votes in the opposition, aside from political motives, were in part due to distaste for any Mexican territòry. The opposing Democrats, with the probable exception of Benton, were dissatisfied with the cession of only New Mexico and Upper California. They would have been glad to acquire more territory, if not the whole of Mexico.

As soon as the Senate had acted, Polk dispatched a special messenger to notify General Butler that the treaty had been ratified.[71] In a few days Senator Sevier and Attorney-General Clifford were sent to Mexico to secure ratification from the Mexican government.[72] They were instructed to point out to the Mexicans that

> Should the war be renewed, the Mexican Government can never again expect to make peace on terms so favorable as those contained in the present Treaty. In the opinion of a very large and increasing number of our fellow citizens, these terms are less favorable to the United States than we had a right to expect. . . . Should the war be renewed, instead of purchasing at a fair price a portion of the territories which we have been obliged to conquer and which are now in our undisturbed possession, and restoring the remainder to Mexico, we shall be compelled to appropriate, without pecuniary compensation, a just and ample indemnity in Mexican territory for all the expenses of the war.[73]

Polk was not only giving the Mexicans information as to what he would do, but also giving some indication of what

---

[70] *American Register*, I, 15-16; Cole, *The Whig Party in the South*, p. 125 n.

[71] Polk's *Diary*, III, 378.

[72] Soon after his appointment Sevier became ill and Clifford was named as his associate. Clifford set out for Mexico at once while Sevier followed in a few days. McCormac, p. 548.

[73] A copy of the instructions to Sevier and Clifford, dated March 18, 1848, may be found in Buchanan's *Works*, VIII, 11.

might have been expected had not Trist upset his plans. If Mexico were wise she would not fail to ratify the treaty.

Meanwhile, comments of leading newspapers in the United States seemed to indicate a favorable reaction to the prospects of peace. According to the Boston *Post*, " the intelligence of the ratification of the treaty . . . diffused general pleasure among our citizens; its confirmation by Mexico is not doubted." [74] The Richmond *Enquirer* and the New Orleans *Picayune* expressed similar sentiments.[75] The *New Englander* severely criticized the treaty, but declared that the case was not " as bad as it might be." " In the long history of conquest and national robbery, since the days of Nimrod, we do not remember anything half so generous." [76] The Detroit *Free Press* had no doubt but that the United States had secured the " best treaty we could get." [77] The *Democratic Review* [78] and the New York *Herald* expressed acquiescence but not enthusiasm. The *Herald* bestowed a benediction on all concerned in the making and ratification of the treaty.

There will be a great cry from some unimportant quarters against this treaty of peace, and against giving up the whole of Mexico, which we might have annexed . . . to this republic . . . but perhaps it is better that we should swallow that country by separate mouthfuls, for fear it might injure our digestive organs. . . . In the meantime we think the Senate has done right—the President has done right—Mr. Trist has done right. . . . [79]

When the New York *Herald* felt disposed to express such sentiments it is evident that the ratification of the Treaty of Guadalupe Hidalgo had sounded the death knell of the press campaign for the absorption of Mexico.

The expansionists in the Senate, however, had not entirely

---

[74] Boston *Post*, 13 March 1848.

[75] Richmond *Enquirer*, 13 March 1848; New Orleans *Picayune*, 19 March 1848.

[76] *New Englander*, VI, 292-294.

[77] Detroit *Free Press*, 17 March 1848.

[78] *Democratic Review*, XXII, 375, 472.

[79] New York *Herald*, 12 March 1848; The *National Era* also had a word of commendation for Trist: " ' Don Nicholas P. Trist,' by his temerity, has probably saved the country and the Administration from the consequences of a most ill-advised measure of the latter—the revocation of the Peace Commission." *National Era*, 9 March 1848.

given up hope pending final action by Mexico. On March 14, an attempt was made in executive session to remove the injunction of secrecy from the proceedings of the Senate on the treaty.[80] Apparently it was expected that if the division of opinion in the Senate became public, Mexico might refuse to accept the amended treaty in the hope of securing better terms. This would reopen the whole question. The attempt failed and no action was taken until the last of May.[81] Debate on the bill for providing additional troops continued. The expansionists explained that an increase in the military forces was necessary in order to induce Mexico to ratify the treaty, or in case of rejection to prosecute the war more vigorously.[82] Perhaps the adherents of extensive annexations would not have been greatly disappointed if there had been a need for the troops. At any rate they intended to be ready for any eventualities. On April 29, the Senate received a message from the President recommending the occupation of Yucatan for the purpose of protecting the white inhabitants. This action had been requested by the Commissioner from Yucatan.[83] This was the signal for a debate in which the expansionists advanced the commercial importance of Yucatan, the danger of English intervention and the dictates of "humanity" as reasons why the United States should enter Yucatan.[84] Whatever may have been the ultimate purposes of Houston, Cass, Dix and the rest in regard to Yucatan or all Mexico,[85] the news of May 17, that the trouble in

---

[80] Polk's *Diary*, III, 385-386.

[81] McCormac, pp. 548-549.

[82] For speeches of Cass, Jefferson Davis and Westcott, see *Cong. Globe, 30th Cong., 1st sess.*, pp. 462, 497, 499. The bill passed the Senate on March 17, 1848, Calhoun being the only Democrat to vote in the negative. *Ibid.*, p. 503.

[83] *Ibid.*, p. 709.

[84] For speeches of Jefferson Davis, Houston, Cass, Bagby and Dix, see *ibid.*, pp. 729, 738, 754, 773, 777-778.

[85] Dodd takes the view that Polk, his cabinet and the expansionists in the Senate intended to use the Yucatan embroglio to reopen the question of the annexation of all Mexico. The case is purely hypothetical, however, and the whole affair was over in less than three weeks after Polk's message was delivered. Dodd, *The West and the War with Mexico*, pp. 168-171; Rippy, pp. 25-26.

Yucatan had been settled put an end to the business.[86] When on June 9, Washington learned that Mexico had ratified the treaty,[87] the movement for the absorption of that country passed into the discard for the time being.

The expansionists were not able to overcome the obstacle presented by the Treaty of Guadalupe Hidalgo. Peace with Mexico on "just and honorable" terms was a contingency which they had not expected and for which they were not prepared. Consequently, when Mexico offered terms which a majority of the American people would undoubtedly consider as satisfactory, most of the expansionists yielded to necessity. Many senators, moreover, lent their support to a treaty which they did not like partly because they desired to frustrate the schemes of the expansionists. The negotiation of the treaty and its acceptance by the President was the beginning of the end; the consent to ratification by the senate furthered the dissolution; and the acceptance of the amended treaty by Mexico, delivered the final blow to the sentiment for the absorption of Mexico.

---

[86] *Cong. Globe., 30th Cong., 1st sess.*, p. 778.
[87] For events in Mexico, see Smith, II, 249-251; Rives, II, 650-655.

CHAPTER V

CONCLUSION

The movement for the absorption of Mexico was no isolated event, nor did it find its origin in the war itself. For about sixty years before that conflict the American people had been looking with interest toward the Southwest, which during the earlier part of the period was controlled by Spain and later by Mexico. During this period the closure of the Mississippi by Spain, the advance of the Americans toward the West and Southwest, and the long debate on the Texas question had created a perennial interest in expansion in the United States. At the same time in order to rationalize land-grabbing tendencies of the Anglo-Saxons in America, propagandists had succeeded in instilling in the minds of many people a number of shibboleths which could always be drawn upon to support practically any scheme of expansion. The catchwords in the expansionist vocabulary included such phrases or ideas as manifest destiny, extension of religious and political freedom, and the checkmating of European machinations in the new world. In 1846, therefore, when the Mexican War began there was already in the United States a rather widespread sentiment which asserted the desirability, the necessity and the inevitability of expansion.

Concerning the sincerity of the expansionists much uncertainty must naturally exist. Nevertheless, some general observations may well be made. In their origin, and thereafter in the minds of many expansionists, professed motives probably had little force in themselves; but were merely used to glorify those acquisitive tendencies which are rooted in human nature. As time went on, however, continued reiteration seems to have produced in the popular mind a sincere belief in the civilizing mission of the United States. Consequently, what might appear to be sheer hypocrisy was in many cases a curious mixture of idealism and greed. Both elements in the mixture were real and it would be difficult indeed to

160

determine which was the stronger. It must be admitted, however, that it was only the expansionists who recognized any validity in arguments based on destiny, freedom and the like. The manifest destiny of the United States was not manifest to those who did not desire that the mission be fulfilled. The conclusion seems to be that the desire created the ideal and the created soon became as great as the creator. Be that as it may, there did exist in the United States in 1846 a strong sentiment for expansion, characterized not only by hypocrisy and sordidness but also by sincerity and idealism.

This being true, it might have been expected that the war would furnish an excellent opportunity for the rapid growth of expansionist sentiment. And so it did to some extent. But the schemes of the imperialists were greatly hindered by a sectional controversy which was beginning to assume ominous proportions in the United States. What was at bottom a naked power issue between two different and opposing economic systems, emerged during the Mexican War as a struggle between the slaveholding South and the free North as to whether territory secured from Mexico should be slave or free. The slavocracy has been acquitted of the traditional charge of having conspired to precipitate the Mexican War in order to extend the area of slavery. But the opinion still persists that slaveholders as a class, once the war had begun, were determined to use the occasion to take as much of Mexico as possible—the more the better—in order to extend their peculiar institution. The other side of the picture is that the anti-slavery forces were interested in preventing the acquisition of large amounts of Mexican territory because they feared the extension of slavery.

This view needs serious modification. It seems that the chief support for the absorption of Mexico came from the North and West and from those whose pro-slavery or anti-slavery bias was not a prime consideration. During the first year of the war there was a general belief that territory taken from Mexico could be occupied by slaveholders. In the same period there developed a fierce sectional controversy between

North and South which threatened to smash the Union or at least prevent the acquisition of any Mexican territory. By the fall of 1847, however, when events in Mexico and the United States seemed to point to the absorption of the former country, much of the explosive material in the slavery issue had been temporarily removed and large plans of expansion could be more easily developed. Then there appeared in quarters where slavery was a major consideration a definite pro-slavery " conspiracy " to prevent the absorption of Mexico and an anti-slavery " conspiracy " to take all Mexican territory available. In both cases the dominant motive seems to have been a conviction that slavery would not and could not be established in such territory, or that if it were, the institution would be weakened thereby. On the part of the slaveholders involved, there was an additional fear of the sectional issue over slavery. Neither " conspiracy " had time to develop its full strength before the end of the war. Had hostilities continued several months longer it is entirely possible that the drive for Mexican territory would have appeared in the guise of an anti-slavery crusade.

It must be admitted at once that there were many slaveholders who were ardent expansionists and many opponents of slavery who protested against extensive additions of Mexican territory. In neither case, and this is more true of the slaveholders, does slavery seem to have been the determining factor. The slaveholding expansionists were for the most part located in the Southwest and were led on by the manifest destiny ideal so prevalent on the frontier. Their attitude differed in no essential respect from that of free states of the West. The inhabitants of the entire West were expansionists first and than pro-slavery or anti-slavery after the empire had been conquered. The anti-slavery opposition to the acquisition of Mexico, although ostensibly based on a protest against the extension of slavery, seems to have been motivated to a considerable extent by the partisan opposition of Whigs to Democratic measures. So far as New England is concerned there was a further distaste for westward expansion which it was thought would weaken the influence of the eastern seabord.

Among the causes for the failure of this country to annex Mexico in 1848, lack of time for expansionist sentiment to develop was probably the most important. The unprecedented action of Nicholas P. Trist is largely responsible for this fact. Even as it was, however, there might have been sufficient demand for annexation in February and March, 1848, to have wrecked the Treaty of Guadalupe Hidalgo had it not been for the opposition of pro-slavery Democrats led by Calhoun. The opposition of Whigs from both slave states and free states was to be expected and could doubtless have been overborne. But the attitude of the Calhounites divided the party committed to expansion in the presence of an opposition which was still for the most part united. Whatever the motives which may be attributed to Trist and to Calhoun and his friends, the fact remains that those who feel that the absorption of Mexico in 1848 would have meant permanent injury to the best interests of the United States, should be extremely grateful to those men. To them not a little credit is due for the fact that Mexico is today an independent nation.

BIBLIOGRAPHY

MANUSCRIPT SOURCES (LIBRARY OF CONGRESS)

Crittenden, John J., Papers.
Donelson, Andrew J., Papers.
McLean, John, Papers.
Marcy, William L., Papers.
Marcy, William L., Private Letter-Book as Secretary of War.
Polk, James K., Papers.
Trist, Nicholas P., Papers.
Van Buren, Martin, Papers.
Webster, Daniel, Papers.

PRINTED SOURCES

COLLECTIONS OF OFFICIAL DOCUMENTS AND TREATIES

Adams, E. D., *British Diplomatic Corespondence Concerning the Republic of Texas, 1838-1846*, Austin, 1918 (reprinted from the *Quarterly* of the Texas State Historical Association, XV, Nos. 3 and 4, and from the *Southwestern Historical Quarterly*, XVI, No. 1–XXI, No. 2, January, 1912–October, 1917).

Congressional Globe, 46 vols. in 110, Washington, 1834-1873.

Hasse, Adelaide R., *Index to United States Documents Relating to Foreign Affairs, 1828-1861*, 3 vols., Washington, 1914-1921.

Garrison, G. P., ed., *Diplomatic Correspondence of the Republic of Texas*, 3 vols., in *Annual Report of the American Historical Association for 1907*, II and *for 1908*, II, Washington, 1908-1911.

Malloy, W. M., comp., *Treaties, Conventions, International Acts, Protocols and Agreements between the United States of America and Other Powers*, 2 vols., Washington, 1910.

Richardson, J. D., ed., *Messages and Papers of the Presidents*, 10 vols., Washington, 1896-1899.

Senate Documents:
    29th Congress, 1st session, No. 1.
    29th Congress, 1st session, No. 337.
    30th Congress, 1st session, No. 52.

Statutes at Large of the United States, 46 vols., Boston and Washington, 1848——.

CORRESPONDENCE, SPEECHES, ETC.

Bancroft, George, *The Life and Letters of* (M. A. De Wolfe Howe editor), 2 vols., New York, 1908.

Buchanan, James, *The Works of* (J. B. Moore editor), 12 vols., Philadelphia and London, 1908-1911.

Calhoun, John C., *Correspondence of* (J. F. Jameson editor), in *Annual Report of the American Historical Association for 1899*, II, Washington, 1900.

Calhoun, John C., *Correspondence Addressed to* (R. P. Brooks and C. S. Boucher editors), in *Annual Report of the American Historical Association for 1929*, Washington, 1930.

165

Calhoun, John C., *The Works of* (R. K. Crallé editor), 6 vols., New York, 1853-1859.

Chase, Salmon P., *The Diary and Correspondence of* (E. G. Bourne editor), in *Annual Report of the American Historical Association for 1902*, II, Washington, 1903.

Davis, Jefferson, *Constitutionalist, His Letters, Papers and Speeches* (Dunbar Rowland editor), 10 vols., Jackson, 1923.

Hunter, Robert M. T., *Correspondence of, 1826-1876* (C. H. Ambler editor), in *Annual Report of the American Historical Association for 1916*, II, Washington, 1918.

Quitman, John A., *Life and Correspondence of* (J. F. H. Claiborne editor), 2 vols., New York, 1860.

Sherman Letters: *Correspondence between General and Senator Sherman from 1837 to 1891* (Rachel S. Thorndike editor), New York, 1894.

Sumner, Charles, *The Works of*, 15 vols., Boston, 1875-1883.

Robert Toombs, Alexander H. Stephens, and Howell Cobb, *The Correspondence of* (U. B. Phillips editor), in *Annual Report of the American Historical Association for 1911*, II, Washington, 1913.

Tyler, Lyon G., *The Letters and Times of the Tylers*, 3 vols., Richmond and Williamsburg, 1884-1896.

Webster, Daniel, *The Works of* (Edward Everett editor), 6 vols., Boston, 1851.

AUTOBIOGRAPHY AND MEMOIRS

Benton, Thomas H., *Thirty Years View*, 2 vols., New York, 1856.

Green, Thomas J., *Journal of the Texian Expedition against Mier*, New York, 1845.

Kenly, John R., *Memoirs of a Maryland Volunteer in the War with Mexico*, Philadelphia, 1873.

Polk, James K., *The Diary of* (Milo M. Quaife editor), 4 vols., Chicago, 1910.

Scott, Winfield, *Autobiography*, New York, 1864.

BIOGRAPHY

Beveridge, A. J., *Abraham Lincoln 1809-1858*, 2 vols., Boston, 1928.

Coleman, Mrs. C., *Life of John J. Crittenden*, 2 vols., Philadelphia, 1871.

Colton, C., *The Last Seven Years of the Life of Henry Clay*, New York, 1856.

Curtis, G. T., *Life of James Buchanan*, 2 vols., New York, 1883.

Johnston, A. M. and Browne, W. H., *Life of Alexander H. Stephens*, Philadelphia, 1878.

Julian, G. W., *The Life of Joshua R. Giddings*, Chicago, 1892.

McCormac, E. I., *James K. Polk*, Berkeley, 1922.

SECONDARY WORKS

Adams, E. D., *British Interests and Activities in Texas, 1838-1846*, Baltimore, 1910.

Adams, E. D., *The Power of Ideals in American History*, New Haven, 1926.

Binkley, W. C., *The Expansionist Movement in Texas, 1836-1850* (University of California Publications in History), Berkeley, 1925.

Boucher, C. S., *In Re that Aggressive Slavocracy*, Austin, 1921.

Cole, A. C., *The Whig Party in the South*, Washington, 1913.

Corwin, E. S., *French Policy and the American Alliance*, Princeton, 1916.

Garrison, G. P., *Westward Extension*, New York, 1906.

Manning, W. R., *Early Diplomatic Relations between the United States and Mexico*, Baltimore, 1916.

McCaleb, W. F., *The Aaron Burr Conspiracy*, New York, 1903.

Pratt, J. W., *The Expansionists of 1812*, New York, 1925.

Reeves, J. S., *American Diplomacy under Tyler and Polk*, Baltimore, 1907.

Rippy, J. F., *The United States and Mexico*, New York, 1926.

Rives, G. L., *The United States and Mexico, 1821-1848*, 2 vols., New York, 1913.

Smith, J. H., *The Annexation of Texas*, New York, 1911.

——, *The War with Mexico*, 2 vols., New York, 1919.

Turner, F. J., *The Frontier in American History*, New York, 1920.

Weinberg, A. K., *Manifest Destiny: a Study of Nationalist Expansionism in American History*, Baltimore, 1935.

Whitaker, A. P., *The Spanish American Frontier: 1783-1795*, Boston, 1927.

ARTICLES

Bourne, E. G., "The Proposed Absorption of Mexico, 1847-1848," *Annual Report of the American Historical Association for 1899*, I, 155-169.

——, "The United States and Mexico, 1847-1848," *American Historical Review*, V, 491-502, April, 1900.

Dodd, W. E., "The West and the War with Mexico," *Journal of the Illinois State Historical Society*, V, 159-172, July, 1912.

Fuller, John D. P., "The Slavery Question and the Movement to Acquire Mexico, 1846-1848," *Mississippi Valley Historical Review*, XXI, 31-48, June, 1934.

Jordan, H. D., "A Politician of Expansion: Robert J. Walker," *Mississippi Valley Historical Review*, XIX, 362-381, December, 1932.

Pratt, J. W., "The Origin of 'Manifest Destiny,'" *American Historical Review*, XXXII, 795-798, July, 1927.

——, "John L. O'Sullivan and Manifest Destiny," *New York History*, XIV, 213-234, July, 1933.

Reeves, J. S., "The Treaty of Guadalupe Hidalgo," *American Historical Review*, X, 309-324, January, 1905.

Sears, L. M., "Nicholas P. Trist, a Diplomat with Ideals," *Mississippi Valley Historical Review*, XI, 85-98, June, 1924.

NEWSPAPERS AND PERIODICALS

(including all those mentioned in the text)

Albany *Argus*.

American Museum (Philadelphia).

American Register (Philadelphia).

Augusta *Constitutionalist*.

Baltimore *American.*
Boston *Atlas.*
Boston *Post.*
Charleston *Courier.*
Charleston *Mercury.*
Chicago *Democrat.*
Cincinnati *Gazette.*
De Bow's Review (New Orleans).
Detroit *Free Press.*
Democratic Review (New York).
Illinois *Globe.*
Illinois *State Register.*
Mobile *Herald.*
Nashville *Clarion.*
Nashville *Union.*
National Era (Washington).
National Intelligencer (Washington).
National Whig (Washington).
New Englander (New Haven).
New Orleans *Bee.*
New Orleans *Commercial Bulletin.*
New Orleans *Commercial Times.*
New Orleans *Mercury.*
New Orleans *Picayune.*
New York *Courier.*
New York *Evening Post.*
New York *Herald.*
New York *Morning News.*
New York *Sun.*
New York *Tribune.*
Niles' Weekly Register (Baltimore).
North American Review (Boston).
Philadelphia *Ledger.*
Princeton (Indiana) *Clarion.*
Richmond *Enquirer.*
Richmond *Whig.*
Southern Literary Messenger (Richmond).
Southern Quarterly Review (Charleston).
St. Louis *Republican.*
St. Louis *Reveille.*

INDEX

169

Giles, Representative, of Maryland, 56.
Great Britain. *See* England.
Green, Thomas J., 69, 70.
Guadalupe Hidalgo, treaty of, 81, 115, 116, 124, 134, 136; and the expansionist movement in the United States, 137, 159; signed, 139-140; received at Washington, 145; in the Senate, 148, 150-156; views of the press, 148-150, 157; attempt to publish proceedings of the Senate, 158; ratified by Mexico, 159.

Hale, John P., and Calhoun, 113 n.; on the Mexican War, 119-120.
Hannegan, Edward A., and Democratic dissensions, 58 n.; on the absorption of Mexico, 131-132, 135 n., 152; and the treaty of peace, 144 n., 151, 152.
Hatcher, George, on motives of the expansionists, 111 n.; and the anti-slavery demand for Mexico, 119 n., 122-123.
Holmes, Isaac, 104.
Hooper, Foster, 72 n.
Houston, Sam, and the expansion of Texas, 18; supports Polk's Mexican policy, 36; on the absorption of Mexico, 107-108, 114, 131 n.; and the Treaty of Guadalupe Hidalgo, 150, 153, 155; occupation of Yucatan, 158.
Hunter, R. M. T., 151.

Illinois *Globe*, on the opposition of slaveholders to expansion, 118.
Illinois *State Register*, and the absorption of Mexico, 21 n., 41, 52, 89; opposes slavery agitation, 59; on opposition of Illinois to the extension of slavery, 59 n.; and foreign intervention, 66; slavery in Mexican territory, 73.
Ingersoll, Charles J., 23-24.

Jackson, Andrew, 19.
Johnson, Cave, 146.
Johnson, David, on slavery and the annexation of Mexico, 85-86, 112 n., 113 n.
Johnson, Governor, of Louisiana, 114.
Johnson, Henry, 116, 153.
Johnson, Reverdy, 55 n.-56 n.; on alleged reasons for absorption of Mexico, 110 n.; changes views on Mexican question, 116, 153.

Lesesne, Joseph W., 60, 65 n., 66.
Lewis, Dixon H., 155 n.
Lieber Francis, 98 n.
Lincoln, Abraham, 115-116.
Louisiana, purchase of, 13.
Lumpkin, Wilson, 51, 85.

McClernand, John A., 41.
McLane, Louis, 110 n.
McLane, Robert, 133 n.
McLean, John, and slavery in Mexican territory, 71; in the campaign of 1848, 90-91.
Mangum, Willie P., 151.
Manifest destiny: and the absorption of Mexico, 10, 50, 52, 135; in the West, 24-25, 31, 41, 48, 114-115, 116, 162; origin of phrase, 25 n.; in New York, 25 n., 31; and Congress, 56, 132-133; in the campaign of 1848, 107-108, 110; nature of sentiment, 160-161.
Marcy, William L., 143, 144, 146.
Mason, John Y., 144, 146.
Merrick, Senator, of Maryland, 23.
Mexican War: causes of, 9, 15-17, 37-38; and expansionist sentiment, 48-49, 52-53; effect on American psychology, 79.
Mexico: early American interest in, 12 ff.; refuses to sell Texas, 15; severs diplomatic relations with the United States, 32; will not receive Slidell, 33-34; refuses Polk's offer to negotiate, 49; effect of refusal, 79-80; annexationist movement in, 83, 88, 89, 93, 95, 107, 138; ratifies Treaty of Guadalupe Hidalgo, 159.
Miller, Washington D., 18.
Missouri Compromise, 71, 76, 77.
Mobile *Herald*, 86-87.
Moderados, 138, 139, 140.